Teach & Test

Math Grade 3

Table of Contents

Introduction 2
Stage a Test 2
Helping Hand Test Strategies 3
Constructed-Response Questions 3
Evaluating the Tests 3
Record Sheet 4
Unit 1: Numeration Part I 5
Unit 1 Test 15
Unit 2: Numeration Part II, Time 19
Unit 2 Test 29
Unit 3: Geometry 33
Unit 3 Test 41
Unit 4: Addition and Subtraction
    Computation 46
Unit 4 Test 56
Midway Review Test Name Grid 60

Midway Review Test Answer Sheet 60
Midway Review Test 61
Unit 5: Multiplication Computation 66
Unit 5 Test 74
Unit 6: Division Computation 78
Unit 6 Test 86
Unit 7: Fractions, Decimals,
    Measurement .90
Unit 7 Test 100
Unit 8: Money, Problem Solving,
    Statistics 104
Unit 8 Test 114
Final Review Test Name Grid 119
Final Review Test Answer Sheet 119
Final Review Test .120
Answer Key 126
Cross-Reference Guide . . . . . .inside back cover

How to Use This Book

1. This book can be used in a home or classroom setting. Read through each unit before working with the student(s). Familiarize yourself with the vocabulary and the skills that are introduced at the top of each unit activity page. Use this information as a guide to help instruct the student(s).

2. Choose a quiet place with little or no interruptions (including the telephone). Talk with the student(s) about the purpose of this book and how you will be working as a team to prepare for standardized tests.

3. As an option, copy the unit test and give it as a pretest to identify weak areas.

4. Upon the completion of each unit, you will find a unit test. Discuss the Helping Hand strategy for test taking featured on the test. Use the example on each test as a chance to show the student(s) how to work through a problem and completely fill in the answer circle. Encourage the student(s) to work independently when possible, but this is a learning time, and questions should be welcomed. A time limit is given for each test. Instruct the student(s) to use the time allowed efficiently, looking back over the answers if possible. Tell him to continue until he sees the stop sign.

5. Record the score on the record sheet on page 4. If a student has difficulty with any questions, use the cross-reference guide on the inside back cover to identify the skills that need to be reviewed.

Teach & Test

Introduction

Now this makes sense—teaching students the skills and strategies that are expected of them before they are tested!

Many students, parents, and teachers are concerned that standardized test scores do not adequately reflect a child's capabilities. This may be due to one or more of the factors italicized below. The purpose of this book is to reduce the negative impact of these, or similar factors, on a student's standardized test scores. The goal is to target those factors and alter their effects as described.

1. *The student has been taught the tested skills but has forgotten them.* This book is divided into units that are organized similarly to third grade textbooks. Instructions for the skill itself are found at the top of each unit activity page, ensuring that the student has been exposed to each key component. The exercises include drill/practice and creative learning activities. Additional activity suggestions can be found in a star burst within the units. These activities require the students to apply the skills that they are practicing.

2. *The student has mastered the skills but has never seen them presented in a test-type format.* Ideally, the skills a student learns at school will be used as part of problem solving in the outside world. For this reason, the skills in this book, and in most classrooms, are not practiced in a test-type format. At the end of each unit in this book, the skills are specifically matched with test questions. In this way, the book serves as a type of "bridge" between the skills that the student(s) has mastered and the standardized test format.

3. *The student is inexperienced with the answer sheet format.* Depending on the standardized test that your school district uses, students are expected to fill in the answer circles completely and neatly. The unit, midway review, and final review tests will help prepare the student(s) for this process.

4. *The student may feel the anxiety of a new and unfamiliar situation.* While testing, students will notice changes in their daily routine: their classroom door will be closed with a "Testing" sign on it, they will be asked not to use the restroom, their desks may be separated, their teacher may read from a script and refuse to repeat herself, etc. To help relieve the stress caused by these changes, treat each unit test in this book as it would be treated at school by following the procedures listed below.

Stage a Test

You will find review tests midway through the book and again at the end of the book. When you reach these points, "stage a test" by creating a real test-taking environment. The procedures listed below coincide with many standardized test directions. The purpose is to alleviate stress, rather than contribute to it, so make this a serious, but calm, event and the student(s) will benefit.

1. Prepare! Have the student(s) sharpen two pencils, lay out scratch paper, and use the restroom.

2. Choose a room with a door that can be closed. Ask a student to put a sign on the door that reads "Testing" and explain that no talking will be permitted after the sign is hung.

3. Direct the student(s) to turn to a specific page but not to begin until the instructions are completely given.

4. Read the instructions at the top of the page and work through the example together. Discuss the Helping Hand strategy that is featured at the top of the page. Have the student(s) neatly and completely fill in the bubble for the example. This is the child's last chance to ask for help!

5. Instruct the student(s) to continue working until the stop sign is reached. If a student needs help reading, you may read each question only once.

Helping Hand Test Strategies

The first page of each test features a specific test-taking strategy that will be helpful in working through most standardized tests. These strategies are introduced and spotlighted one at a time so that they will be learned and remembered internally. Each will serve as a valuable test-taking tool, so discuss them thoroughly.

The strategies include:

- Read all of the choices before you answer.
- When you are unsure, cross out the answers you know are incorrect and make your best guess from those that are left.
- With picture answers, cover some of the choices so you see only one picture at a time.
- Sometimes the correct answer is not given. Fill in the circle for NG if no answer is correct.
- When using scratch paper, copy carefully.
- Compare the answer choices. Some answer choices may look very similar.
- Use your time wisely. If something seems difficult, skip it and come back to it later.
- Always read the question twice. Does your answer make sense?

Constructed-Response Questions

You will find the final question of each test is written in a different format called constructed response. This means that students are not provided with answer choices, but are instead asked to construct their own answers. The objective of such an "open-ended" type of question is to provide students with a chance to creatively develop reasonable answers. It also provides an insight to a student's reasoning and thinking skills. As this format is becoming more accepted and encouraged by standardized test developers, students will be "ahead of the game" by practicing such responses now.

Evaluating the Tests

Two types of questions are included in each test. The unit tests and the midway review test each consist of 20 multiple-choice questions, and the final review test consists of 30 multiple-choice questions. All tests include a constructed-response question which requires the student(s) to construct and sometimes support an answer. Use the following procedures to evaluate a student's performance on each test.

1. Use the answer key found on pages 126–128 to correct the tests. Be sure the student(s) neatly and completely filled in the answer circles.

2. Record the scores on the record sheet found on page 4. If the student(s) incorrectly answered any questions, use the cross-reference guide found on the inside back cover to help identify the skills the student(s) needs to review. Each test question references the corresponding activity page.

3. Scoring the constructed-response questions is somewhat subjective. Discuss these questions with the student(s). Sometimes it is easier for the student(s) to explain the answer verbally. Help the student to record his or her thoughts as a written answer. If the student(s) has difficulty formulating a response, refer back to the activity pages using the cross-reference guide. Also review the star burst activity found in the unit which also requires the student(s) to formulate an answer.

4. Discuss the test with the student(s). What strategies were used to answer the questions? Were some questions more difficult than others? Was there enough time? What strategies did the student(s) use while taking the test?

Record Sheet

Record a student's score for each test by drawing a star or placing a sticker below each item number that was correct. Leave the incorrect boxes empty as this will allow you to visually see any weak spots. Review and practice those missed skills, then retest only the necessary items.

Unit 1

1	2	3	4	5	6	7	8	9	10	11	12	13	14	15	16	17	18	19	20

Unit 2

1	2	3	4	5	6	7	8	9	10	11	12	13	14	15	16	17	18	19	20

Unit 3

1	2	3	4	5	6	7	8	9	10	11	12	13	14	15	16	17	18	19	20

Unit 4

1	2	3	4	5	6	7	8	9	10	11	12	13	14	15	16	17	18	19	20

Midway Review Test

1	2	3	4	5	6	7	8	9	10	11	12	13	14	15	16	17	18	19	20

Unit 5

1	2	3	4	5	6	7	8	9	10	11	12	13	14	15	16	17	18	19	20

Unit 6

1	2	3	4	5	6	7	8	9	10	11	12	13	14	15	16	17	18	19	20

Unit 7

1	2	3	4	5	6	7	8	9	10	11	12	13	14	15	16	17	18	19	20

Unit 8

1	2	3	4	5	6	7	8	9	10	11	12	13	14	15	16	17	18	19	20

Final Review Test

1	2	3	4	5	6	7	8	9	10	11	12	13	14	15	16	17	18	19	20

21	22	23	24	25	26	27	28	29	30

Name

Finding ordinal places

The **ordinal** of an object is found by counting its place in line. To count ordinal numbers, use first (1st), second (2nd), third (3rd), etc.

Write the missing numbers on the tickets to show their order. Then use the tickets to help you find the answers at the bottom.

A. 1st | 2nd | 3rd | 4th

B. 18th | 19th | 20th | 25th

C. 79th | 83rd | 88th

D. If you are holding the eighth ticket, how many people are ahead of you?

E. You are 14th in line, and there are 19 people in line, how many people are behind you?

F. You are 11th and your friend is 13th. Which place is the person between you?

Name

Comparing picture groups

One way to compare numbers is by their value. Words like more, greater, and greatest indicate the larger number. Less, least, and fewer indicate the smaller number.

Finish each picture as described.

In Our Classroom

There are 4 more pencils than crayons on the desk. Draw them.

There are 3 fewer books than jars on the shelf. Draw them.

There are the same number of balls as there are jacks. Draw them.

There are 4 more apples than staplers on the table. Draw them.

On the Beach

There are 5 more fish than birds. Draw them.

There are 2 less starfish than there are crabs. Draw them.

There are an equal number of shovels and buckets. Draw them.

There are 3 more shells than there are sandcastles. Draw them.

Identifying place value using tens

Two-digit numbers have two parts: the tens column (or place) and the ones column (or place). The columns determine a number's place value. The number can also be shown using tens blocks ▭▭▭▭▭ and ones blocks □.

Count the tens and ones. Write the number two ways.

	tens	ones
=	3	5

= 35

A.

	tens	ones
=		

=

B.

	tens	ones
=		

=

C.

	tens	ones
=		

=

D.

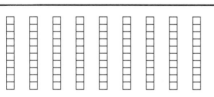

	tens	ones
=		

=

E.

	tens	ones
=		

=

F.

	tens	ones
=		

=

G.

	tens	ones
=		

=

Name

Identifying place value using hundreds

Three-digit numbers have three parts: the hundreds column (place), the tens column (place), and the ones column (place). The number can also be shown using blocks:

 hundreds    tens   ones

Count the hundreds, tens, and ones. Write the number two ways.

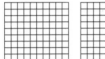 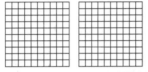

H	T	O
2	4	1

=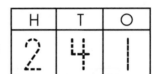

A.

H	T	O

=

B.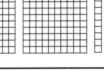

H	T	O

=

C.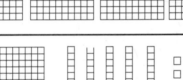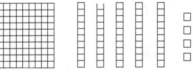

H	T	O

=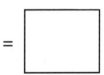

D.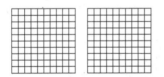

H	T	O

=

E.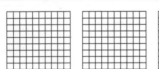

H	T	O

=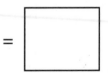

F.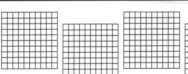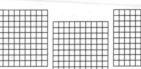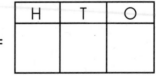

H	T	O

=

G.

H	T	O

=

Identifying place value using thousands

Another place value column is the thousands. The thousands place is sometimes separated from the hundreds with a comma (,), and it makes a fourth digit. To show one thousand using blocks, we use 10 hundreds, so it looks like this:

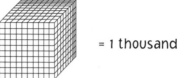 = 1 thousand

Write each 4-digit number two ways.

     =

Th	H	T	O
1	3	0	4

= 1,304

A.

  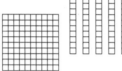 =

Th	H	T	O

= _____,_____

B.

  =

Th	H	T	O

= _____,_____

C.

 =

Th	H	T	O

= _____,_____

D.

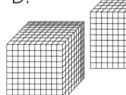 =

Th	H	T	O

= _____,_____

E.

  =

Th	H	T	O

= _____,_____

Name

Writing in expanded form

Our place value system is based on groups of ten. This chart shows how the ones, tens, hundreds, and thousands relate to each other.

1,000	100	10	1
1 thousand = 10 hundreds	1 hundred = 10 tens	1 ten = 10 ones	

This chart is helpful when writing numbers in expanded form. For example:

$$3,649 = 3,000 + 600 + 40 + 9$$

Write each number in expanded form.

		1,000		100		10		1
	9,516 =	9,000	+	500	+	10	+	6
A.	2,358 =		+		+		+	
B.	1,407 =		+		+		+	
C.	921 =		+		+		+	
D.	7,800 =		+		+		+	
E.	3,264 =		+		+		+	
F.	5,182 =		+		+		+	
G.	614 =		+		+		+	
H.	4,073 =		+		+		+	
I.	9,530 =		+		+		+	

Name

naming numbers to 99

Numbers can be written as words, as well as numerals.

Find the written name for each number. Use the matching letters to answer this fact.

Where does the male emperor penguin keep the eggs warm?

___ ___   ___ ___ ___   ___ ___ ___ ___ ___
74 19   46 93 36   21 52 76 62 85

ninety-three	I	sixty-two	T	forty-six	H
fifty-nine	R	seventy-four	O	fifty-two	E
nineteen	N	eighty-five	!	twenty-one	F
seventy-six	E	thirty-six	S	ninety	V

Counting order

To use counting order, increase the ones place by one. Follow the pattern as shown. The tens place will not change until you reach 9 and the hundreds place will not change until you reach 99.

Count by ones. Fill in the missing numbers.

71	72	73							
				85			88		
	92				96				100

321	322				326				330
		333				337			
341				345					

671					676				680
		683							
691				695					700

	882			885				889	
			894					899	
901	902				906				

Teach & Test Math: Grade 3

Name

Skip counting

Skip counting means following a given pattern as you count. You are probably used to counting by 2s, 5s, and 10s. Use the number line to "skip" the given number of times:

Count by 5s.

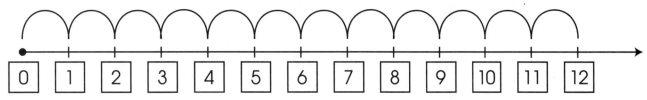

Color the number boxes to show skip counting.

A. Start at 0 and count by 4s.

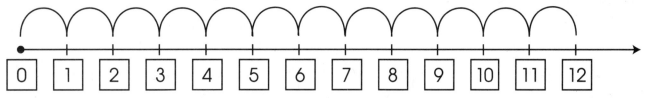

B. Start at 0 and count by 6s.

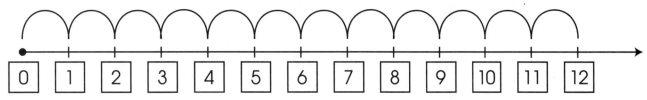

C. Start at 33 and count by 3s.

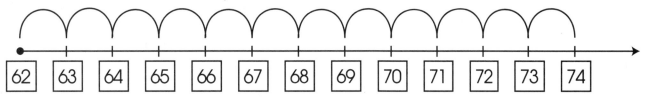

D. Start at 62 and count by 2s.

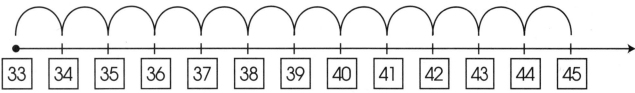

E. Start at 84 and count by 4s.

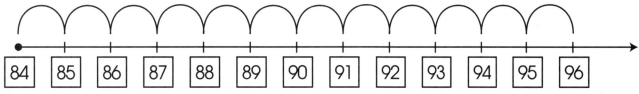

Name

More skip counting

To skip count without a number line, try the directions below. Counting by 4s . . .

1. Make 4 marks on your paper.
2. Touch each mark as you count to yourself.
3. When you reach the last mark, the number you say should be recorded.
4. Make 4 more marks.
5. Continue counting from where you left off to get another multiple of 4.
6. Repeat steps 4 and 5.

| | | | | | | | | | | | | | | | |
1 2 3 (4) 5 6 7 (8) 9 10 11 (12) 13 14 15 (16)

Fill in the empty spaces. Use the marks to help you count and record your answers.

A. Count by threes.

B. Count by sixes.

C. Count by twos.

D. Count by sevens.

E. Count by nines.

F. Count by fives.

Name _____

Read or listen to the question. Fill in the circle beside the best answer.

☐ Example:
Which is another way to name 2,941?

(A) 2 hundreds, 9 tens, 4 thousands, 1 one

(B) 2 thousands, 9 hundreds, 4 tens, 1 one

(C) 2 ones, 9 thousands, 4 hundreds, 1 ten

(D) 2 thousands, 9 ones, 4 tens, 1 hundred

Read all of the choices before you answer.

Answer: B because the place value digits match.

Now try these. You have 20 minutes. Continue until you see STOP .

---

1. Your dog is ninth in line for a bath. How many other dogs are in line ahead of your dog?

six	seven	eight	nine
(A)	(B)	(C)	(D)

---

2. Which set of numbers shows the correct counting order?

(A) 218, 217, 214, 215   (A) 212, 213, 214, 215

(C) 210, 211, 213, 214   (D) 213, 212, 215, 216

---

3. 4,602 = _____

(A) 4 hundreds, 6 tens, 2 ones

(B) 46 thousands, 2 ones

(C) 4 thousands, 6 hundreds, 2 ones

(D) 4602 thousands

Unit 1 Test

4. Which group shows four more spoons than forks?

Ⓐ Ⓐ Ⓐ Ⓐ

5. How would you write 91 in word form?

nineteen	ninety	nine	ninety-one
Ⓐ	Ⓑ	Ⓒ	Ⓓ

6. Which of these numbers has a 2 in the tens place and 7 in the ones place?

472	3,627	2,700	720
Ⓐ	Ⓑ	Ⓒ	Ⓓ

7. How many tens are in 36?

3	13	6	16
Ⓐ	Ⓑ	Ⓒ	Ⓓ

8. Which picture shows counting by fours?

Ⓐ Ⓑ Ⓒ Ⓓ

9. You are between two friends in line. You are fifteenth in line. What numbers are your friends?

Ⓐ fourteenth, sixteenth   Ⓑ sixteenth, seventeenth

Ⓒ thirteenth, fourteenth   Ⓓ fifteenth, sixteenth

GO ON ▷

10. What number is between 25 and 35 when you count by fives?

30	20	40	45
Ⓐ	Ⓑ	Ⓒ	Ⓓ

11. Which shows 5000 + 400 + 20?

2,450	2,045	4,520	5,420
Ⓐ	Ⓑ	Ⓒ	Ⓓ

12. What number comes before 298?

299	290	293	297
Ⓐ	Ⓑ	Ⓒ	Ⓓ

13. Which number equals fifty-eight?

580	58	850	85
Ⓐ	Ⓑ	Ⓒ	Ⓓ

14. Which number is named?

I have a 5 in the ones place and a 7 in the hundreds place.

570	507	705	750
Ⓐ	Ⓑ	Ⓒ	Ⓓ

15. Which number has a five in the hundreds place and a nine in the ones place?

905	590	509	950
Ⓐ	Ⓑ	Ⓒ	Ⓓ

16. Counting by threes, what number comes after 21?

20	22	23	24
Ⓐ	Ⓑ	Ⓒ	Ⓓ

GO ON ➡

17. Look at the lunch plates. Mark the statement that is true.

Ⓐ All of the plates have an equal number of apples.

Ⓑ There are more plates with hot dogs than there are plates without hot dogs.

Ⓒ There are less plates with pickles than there are plates without pickles.

Ⓓ The greatest number of grapes is on the first plate.

18. What number is missing.

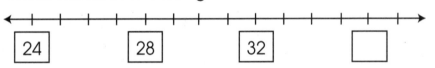

| 24 | | 28 | | 32 | | |

Ⓐ 33   Ⓑ 34
Ⓒ 35   Ⓓ 36

19. Which number shows a 7 in the thousands place?

7,143   1,743   4,173   3,437
Ⓐ   Ⓑ   Ⓒ   Ⓓ

20. What is the correct number?

Ⓐ 2,040   Ⓑ 240
Ⓒ 24   Ⓓ 204

Choose any 4-digit number. Write its name two different ways.

STOP

Name

naming larger numbers in word form

You can use the place value columns to help you write a number's name in word form. It looks like this:

H	T	O
6	4	1

= six hundred forty-one

Th	H	T	O
3	2	1	8

= three thousand, two hundred eighteen

Read each number's name in word form. Then color its matching number on the chicken's nest or the egg.

A. six thousand, nine hundred eleven

B. four thousand, seventy-three

C. nine thousand, two hundred seven

D. eight hundred thirty-nine

E. nine thousand, six hundred one

F. eight thousand, three hundred ninety

G. four hundred seventeen

H. five thousand, eighty-two

I. four hundred seventy

J. three thousand, five hundred twelve

K. six thousand, nine hundred fourteen

Name

naming even/odd numbers   Unit 2

Even numbers end in 0, 2, 4, 6, or 8. **Odd numbers** end in 1, 3, 5, 7, or 9.
Use only the ones column to determine whether a number is even or odd.

Help the frogs leap to victory! Decide whether each number in the pond is even or odd. Record the numbers on the lily pads above the "even" and "odd" frogs. The first frog to fill his path is the winner!

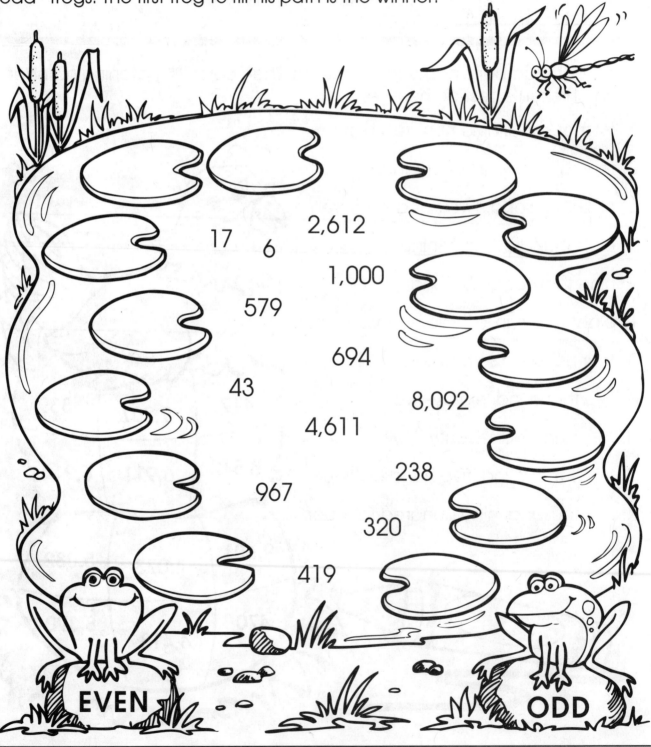

17   6   2,612

1,000

579

694

43

8,092

4,611

967

238

320

419

EVEN   ODD

20

Name

Rounding to the nearest ten

Rounding is one way to estimate or find a close, but not exact, answer.

When rounding to the nearest ten, use these rules:

If the number has 0, 1, 2, 3, or 4 in the ones place, you will round down to the nearest ten.

If the number has 5, 6, 7, 8, or 9 in the ones place, you will round up to the nearest ten.

Round each number to the nearest ten. Write your answer on the lower part of the kite.

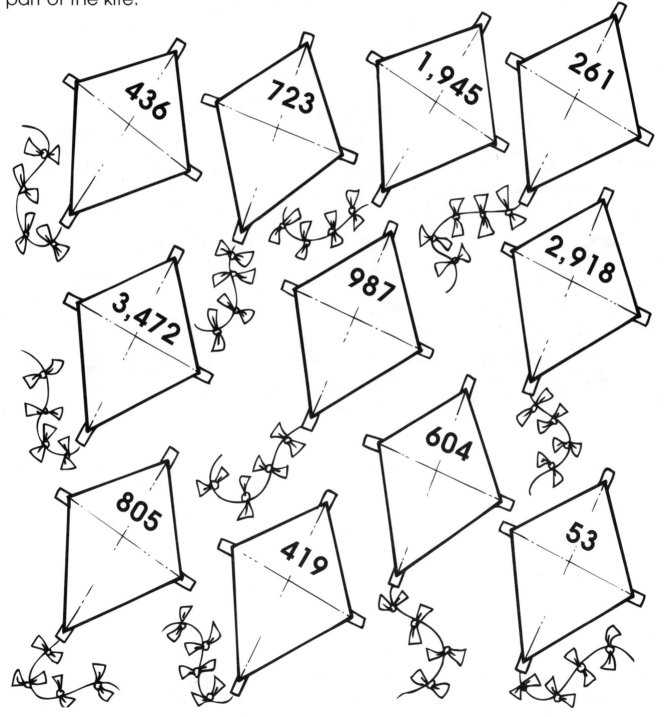

Rounding to the nearest hundred

When rounding to the nearest hundred, use these rules:

1. Look at the tens place.
2. If the number in the tens place is 0, 1, 2, 3, or 4, round down.
3. If the number in the tens place is a 5, 6, 7, 8, or 9, round up.

You have discovered a hidden treasure! A group of pirates is close behind, and you only have time to estimate the value in each treasure chest. Round these amounts to the nearest hundred.

22

Name

Comparing numbers

Comparing numbers means deciding which number is the greatest and which number is the least. The symbol › means greater than and the symbol ‹ means less than. Use these steps to compare:

1. Are the number of digits the same? If not, the number with the most digits is the largest.

2. If the number of digits is the same, begin with the digit on the left. Which number has a larger digit? That is the greater number.

3. If the digits are the same, move to the next place and find the larger number.

671 $<$ 2,318

This number has more digits, so it is greater.

564 $>$ 372

5 is greater.

671 $>$ 619

Same, so go to the next digit. 7 is greater than 1.

Write > or < to compare the numbers.

A.

317 ◯ 1,198

982 ◯ 918

2,479 ◯ 3,923

176 ◯ 134

463 ◯ 9,502

803 ◯ 850

1,601 $>$ 987

B.

298 ◯ 300

761 ◯ 760

4,395 ◯ 4,217

512 ◯ 514

6,330 ◯ 3,630

29 ◯ 30

Name

Ordering numbers

To find the order of numbers, compare their place value columns. Use the steps on page 23.

Order from greatest to least:

The same in the hundreds, so move to the tens!

347   (3)

268   (4)—The least because it has a 2 in the hundreds place.

363   (2)—The second greatest because its tens place is bigger.

1,619   (1)—The greatest because it has 4 digits

Write the numbers in order from greatest to least.

A.

172	905	730	340

_____ , _____ , _____ , _____

B.

1,170	2,314	800	512

_____ , _____ , _____ , _____

C.

982	4,000	960	6,000

_____ , _____ , _____ , _____

D.

401	472	436	490

_____ , _____ , _____ , _____

greatest **952**   2nd greatest **308**   3rd greatest **76**   least **15**

Write the numbers in order from least to greatest.

E.

87	107	71	17

_____ , _____ , _____ , _____

F.

96	906	600	19

_____ , _____ , _____ , _____

G.

1,900	2,700	7,000	4,350

_____ , _____ , _____ , _____

H.

620	6,200	200	2,600

_____ , _____ , _____ , _____

Name

The minute hand on a clock is the long hand. It takes 5 minutes to move from one number on the clock to the next. Therefore, we count by fives as the minute hand moves. To read this clock, we say . . .

 20 minutes past 3:00

3:20

 40 minutes past 9:00

9:40

Write the time two ways.

A.

 | 25 | minutes past | 10:00 |

10:25

 | ☐ | minutes past | ☐ : ☐ |

☐ : ☐

 | ☐ | minutes past | ☐ : ☐ |

☐ : ☐

 | ☐ | minutes past | ☐ : ☐ |

☐ : ☐

 | ☐ | minutes past | ☐ : ☐ |

☐ : ☐

B.

| ☐ | minutes past | ☐ : ☐ |

☐ : ☐

| ☐ | minutes past | ☐ : ☐ |

☐ : ☐

| ☐ | minutes past | ☐ : ☐ |

☐ : ☐

| ☐ | minutes past | ☐ : ☐ |

☐ : ☐

| ☐ | minutes past | ☐ : ☐ |

☐ : ☐

naming time in other ways

Time can be named in other ways. Do you recognize these phrases?

noon
midnight

15 minutes past 4:00
quarter after 4:00
quarter past 4:00

30 minutes past 4:00
half past 4:00

45 minutes past 4:00
quarter till 5:00
quarter to 5:00

Write the time using one of the phrases above.

A.

B.

C.

Draw the hands on the clocks to show the given times.

D.

half past 7:00

E.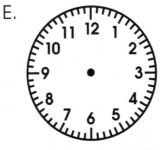

quarter to 8:00

F.

midnight

G.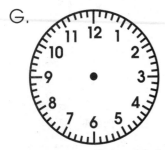

quarter after 3:00

H.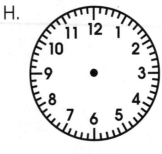

noon

I.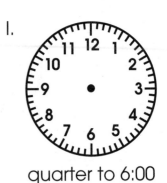

quarter to 6:00

26

Using time throughout the day

Unit 2

The hour hand on the clock takes 60 minutes to move from one number to another. There are 24 hours in a day, so the hour hand passes each number two times every day. This can be confusing, so we name the first 12 hours AM and the second 12 hours PM. It looks like this:

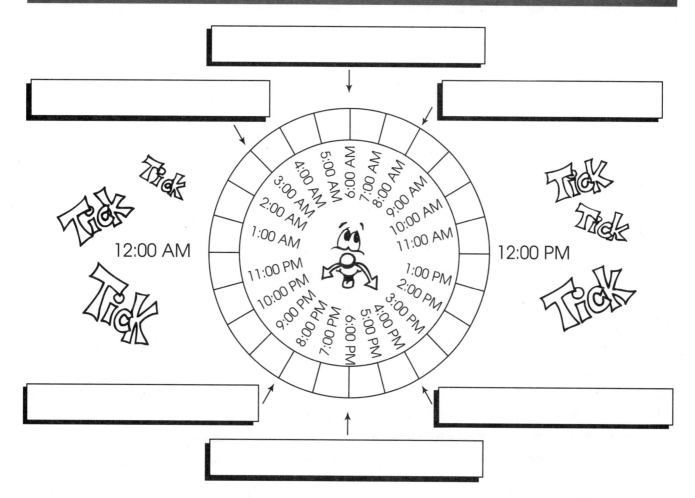

12:00 AM

12:00 PM

Add these daily events to the chart above:

I am asleep.

I go to bed.

I wake up.

I get home from school.

School starts.

I eat dinner.

Name

Calculating elapsed time

To calculate elapsed time, or time that has passed, try these steps:

The school play started at 3:00. It lasted 2 hours 10 minutes. What time did it end?

Step 1: Start at 3:00. Add the hours.

Step 2: Add the minutes.

It will end at 5:10.

The strings concert began at 4:00 and ended at 5:35. How long did the concert last?

Step 1: Start at 4:00. Count the hours.

Step 2: Count the minutes.

It lasted 1 hour 35 minutes.

Use the clocks to help you find the elapsed time.

A. Harry rode his bike from 4:00 to 4:50. How long did he ride his bike?

B. Jeff's game started at 2:00. It ended at 3:40. How long did the game last?

C. Zoe's favorite movie starts at 7:15. It will last for 2 hours and 5 minutes. What time will the movie end?

D. Pollo's cat disappeared at 3:10. Pollo found him at 4:20. How long was his cat lost?

E. The train leaves for New York at 8:05. The ride is 3 hours 10 minutes long. What time will the train arrive in New York?

Write your own problem using elapsed time. Then show the times on the clocks.

Name

Read or listen to the question. Fill in
the circle beside the best answer.

❑ Example:
Emmie is making brownies. She puts them in
the oven at 2:05. They should bake for 15
minutes. What time will she take them out?

2:35   2:30   2:25   2:20
Ⓐ   Ⓑ   Ⓒ   Ⓓ

When you are
unsure, cross out
the answers you
know are incorrect
and make your best
guess from those
that are left.

Answer: D because we start at 2:05 and
move the minute hand 15 more minutes.

Now try these. You have 20 minutes. Continue until you see STOP .

---

1. Which of these numbers is equal to two thousand, six hundred
ninety-two?

6,922   2,692   9,692   6,902
Ⓐ   Ⓑ   Ⓒ   Ⓓ

---

2. Which is an even number?

609   427   306   991
Ⓐ   Ⓑ   Ⓒ   Ⓓ

---

3. Round the numbers in the box to the nearest
ten. How many are rounded to 60?

| 57 | 61 | 54 | 56 |

Ⓐ 1   Ⓑ 2
Ⓒ 3   Ⓓ 4

---

4. Which number would be rounded to 400?

426   481   498   470
Ⓐ   Ⓑ   Ⓒ   Ⓓ

GO ON ▷

5. How many numbers in the box are greater than 362?

| 1,005 | 390 | 280 | 619 | 300 |

(A) 2   (B) 3

(C) 4   (D) 5

6. Which group of numbers is ordered from least to greatest?

(A) 780; 920; 6,300; 4,900

(B) 4,900; 920; 6,300; 780

(C) 780; 6,300; 920; 4,900

(D) 780; 920; 4,900; 6,300

7. What time is shown on the clock?

(A) 7:55   (B) 7:05

(C) 7:15   (D) 8:00

8. Which clock shows quarter till twelve?

(A)   (B)   (C)   (D)

9. How many hours are in 1 ½ days?

12   24   36   48

(A)   (B)   (C)   (D)

10. Round 154 to the nearest ten.

100   150   160   170

(A)   (B)   (C)   (D)

GO ON

Unit 2 Test

11. Max read the clock on his wall. It showed 8:35. "Good! My favorite show starts in 15 minutes!" he said. What time does Max's show start?

8:50	8:45	8:20	8:00
Ⓐ	Ⓑ	Ⓒ	Ⓓ

12. Which word form means 4,375?

Ⓐ four hundred thirty

Ⓑ fourteen thousand, seventy-five

Ⓒ forty-three thousand

Ⓓ four thousand, three hundred seventy-five

13. Which box contains four odd numbers?

12 36	41 95	76 45	19 98
71 99	37 89	31 88	63 56
Ⓐ	Ⓑ	Ⓒ	Ⓓ

14. What is $749 rounded to the nearest hundred?

$800	$750	$700	$740
Ⓐ	Ⓑ	Ⓒ	Ⓓ

15. Which group of numbers is ordered from greatest to least?

Ⓐ 875, 963, 914

Ⓑ 963, 875, 914

Ⓒ 875, 914, 963

Ⓓ 963, 914, 875

GO ON

Unit 2 Test

16. Which greater than/less than statement is true?

738 > 790   2,414 < 980   643 < 690   176 > 1,103

  (A)   (B)   (C)   (D)

17. Which clock shows 1:35?

  (A)   (B)   (C)   (D)

18. What time is shown on the clock?

(A) quarter past 2:00   (B) quarter till 2:00

(C) quarter till 3:00   (D) noon

19. Which statement is most reasonable to do on Saturday?

(A) We eat breakfast at 7:00 p.m.   (B) We wake up at 7:35 a.m.

(C) We go to sleep at 8:45 a.m.   (D) We eat dinner at 6:15 a.m.

20. Which time is different from the others?

8:30   half past eight   quarter till nine

  (A)   (B)   (C)   (D)

Write a time story problem with an answer equal to 2:25. Be sure to give a time that something begins and how long it lasts.

STOP

Name

Identifying spatial figures   Unit 3

Spatial figures are solids that take up space. Below are some spatial figures. The flat side of a figure is called a face.

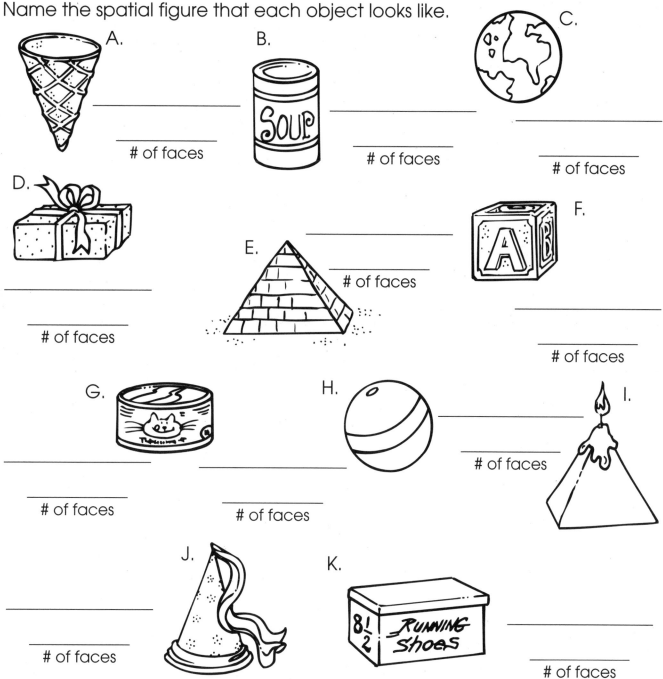

cube
(6 faces)   sphere   rectangular prism
(6 faces)   cone
(1 face)   pyramid
(5 faces)   cylinder
(2 faces)

Name the spatial figure that each object looks like.

A.
_____
_____ # of faces

B.
_____
_____ # of faces

C.
_____
_____ # of faces

D.
_____
_____ # of faces

E.
_____
_____ # of faces

F.
_____
_____ # of faces

G.
_____
_____ # of faces

H.
_____
_____ # of faces

I.

J.
_____
_____ # of faces

K.
_____
_____ # of faces

Name

Identifying parts of shapes

You know that a square has four sides, but did you know that it also has four line segments, four angles, four points, and two sets of parallel lines?

endpoint   endpoint

line segment

closed
curve

angle

parallel lines

Use the pictures above to complete the chart for each shape.

Shape	# Line Segments	# Endpoints	# Angles	Any Parallel Lines?	Any Closed Curves?
A. 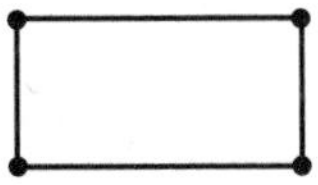					
B. 					
C. 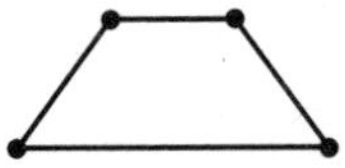					
D. 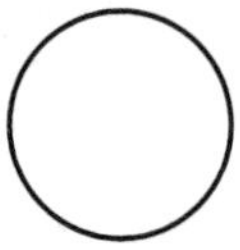					
E. 					
F. 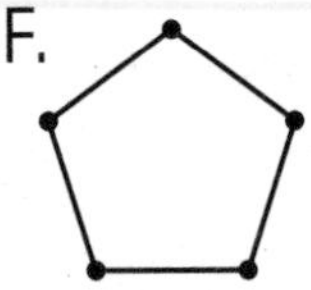					
G. 					

Labeling congruency and movements

Unit 3

Congruent means two shapes are exactly the same in size and shape. The congruent figures may look different because their positions are different. The change in direction is called movement, and there are three types:

slide

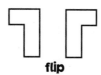

flip

turn (rotate)

Decide if each set of shapes are congruent. If they are, label the movement. If they are not congruent, write **no**.

A.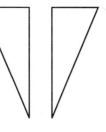

_____

B.

_____

C.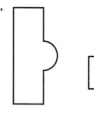

_____

D.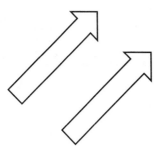

_____

E.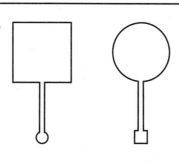

_____

F.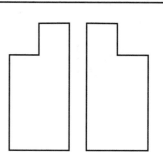

_____

G.

_____

H.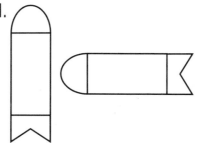

_____

I.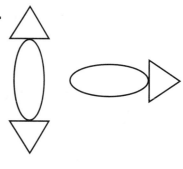

_____

Identifying symmetry

A **line of symmetry** is a line that divides a figure into two identical parts. These are lines of symmetry:

Draw a line of symmetry for each object.

  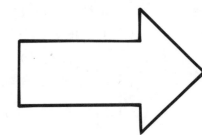

Draw 2 lines of symmetry for each figure.

Draw another figure that has 2 lines of symmetry.

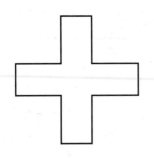 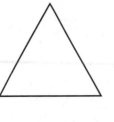 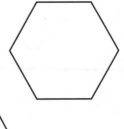

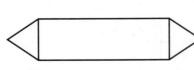 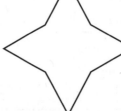

Calculating perimeter

The **perimeter** (P) of a figure is the distance around that figure. The perimeter is measured in units, which may be inches, centimeters, miles, etc. To find the perimeter, add all the sides together.

Find the perimeter of each figure. Label your answer in the units indicated.

A.

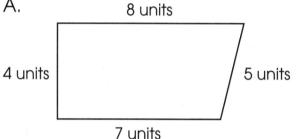

P = _____

B.

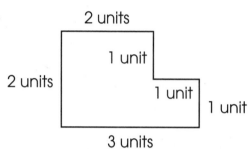

P = _____

C.

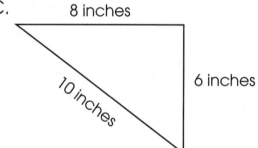

P = _____

D.

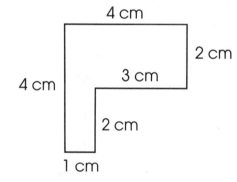

P = _____

E.

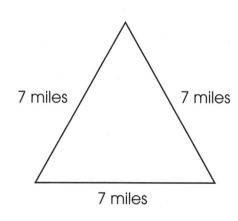

P = _____

F.

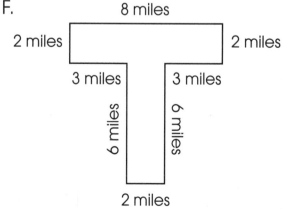

P = _____

Calculating area

Area is the number of square units it takes to cover the surface of a figure. To calculate area, it is easiest to use grid paper as shown. Then count the number of squares it takes to cover the shape. It looks like this:

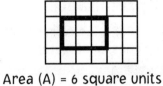

Area (A) = 6 square units

Find the area of each figure.

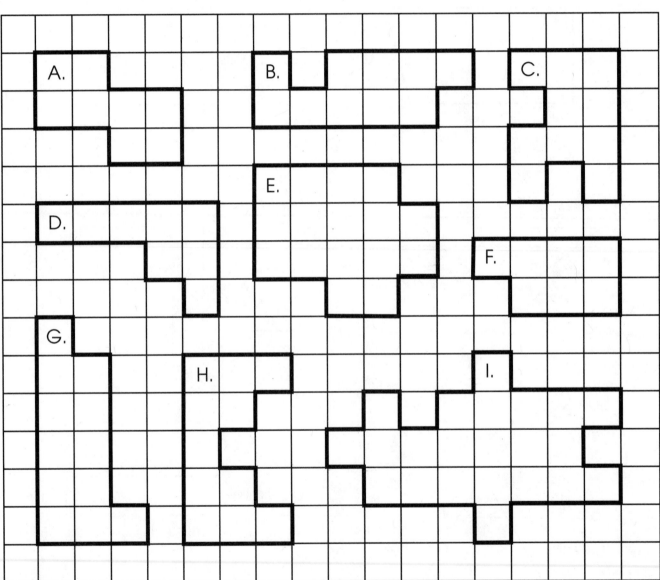

A. A = _____ sq. cm   B. A = _____ sq. cm   C. A = _____ sq. cm

D. A = _____ sq. cm   E. A = _____ sq. cm   F. A = _____ sq. cm

G. A = _____ sq. cm   H. A = _____ sq. cm   I. A = _____ sq. cm

Name

Calculating volume

Volume is the amount of space there is in a solid figure. We use cubes to imagine filling in the figure, and we label our answers in cubic units. Here's how it looks:

Volume =
6 cubic units

Volume =
9 cubic units

The abbreviation for cubic centimeter = cu. cm

Find the volume of each figure. Label your answer in cubic units.

A.

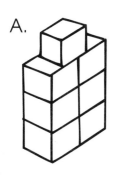

_____

B.

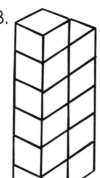

_____

C.

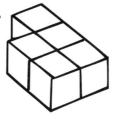

_____

D.

_____

E.

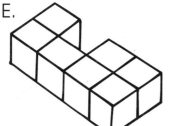

_____

F.

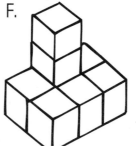

_____

G.

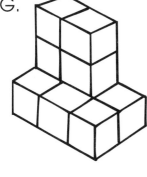

_____

H.

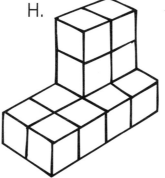

_____

I.

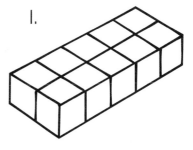

_____

Name

Predicting patterns   Unit 3

By studying a given picture, you can determine its pattern and predict what will come next.

Continue the pattern with three more pictures.

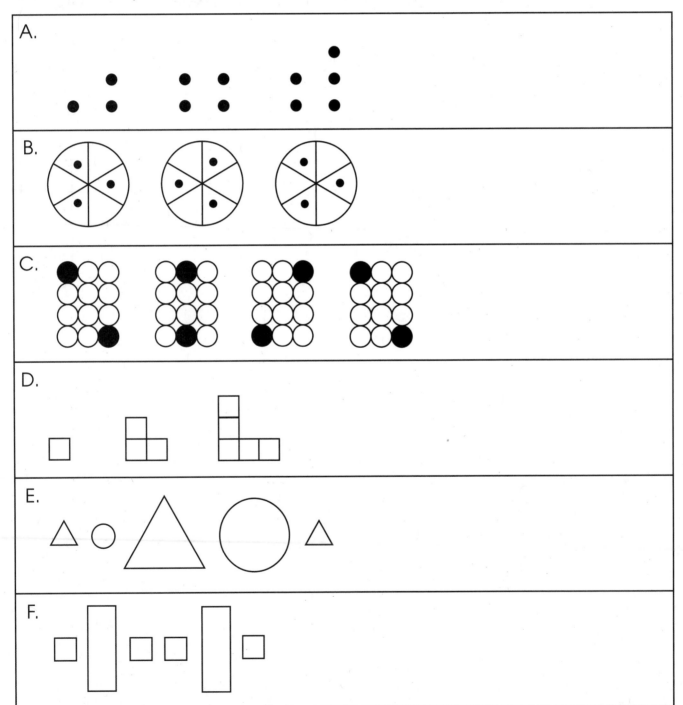

Name

Geometry

Read or listen to the question. Fill in the circle beside the best answer.

◻ **Example:**
How many of the shapes in the box are cones?

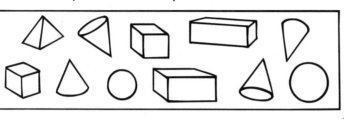

2	3	4	5
Ⓐ	Ⓑ	Ⓒ	Ⓓ

Answer: C

With picture answers, cover some of the choices so you see only one picture at a time.

Now try these. You have 20 minutes. Continue until you see (STOP).

---

1. This object is the shape of a

_____.

- Ⓐ rectangular prism
- Ⓑ sphere
- Ⓒ pyramid
- Ⓓ cylinder

---

2. Which shape has two more angles than a square?

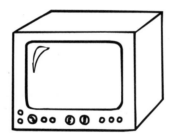

Ⓐ	Ⓑ	Ⓒ	Ⓓ

---

3. Which two shapes are congruent?

 1   2   3 4

- Ⓐ 1, 2
- Ⓑ 3, 4
- Ⓒ 1, 3
- Ⓓ 2, 4

GO ON ⟹

4. Which figure shows a line of symmetry?

Ⓐ Ⓑ Ⓒ Ⓓ

5. Find the perimeter of the figure.

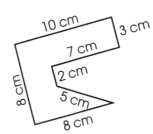

Ⓐ 30 cm   Ⓑ 43 cm

Ⓒ 38 cm   Ⓓ 33 cm

6. Find the area of the figure.

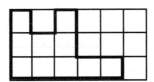

Ⓐ 10 sq. cm   Ⓑ 12 sq. cm

Ⓒ 8 sq. cm   Ⓓ 13 sq. cm

7. Mark the figure with a volume equal to 8 cubic units.

   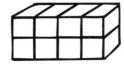

Ⓐ Ⓑ Ⓒ Ⓓ

8. Which figure would come next in the pattern?

Ⓐ a figure whose volume = 6 cu. units

Ⓑ a figure whose volume = 7 cu. units

Ⓒ a figure whose volume = 8 cu. units

Ⓓ a figure whose volume = 9 cu. units

GO ON ⟹

9. Which figure has no line segments?

Ⓐ　　　Ⓑ　　　Ⓒ　　　Ⓓ

10. A sphere is most like which of these objects?

Ⓐ　　　Ⓑ　　　Ⓒ　　　Ⓓ

11. Which figure or object is shaped like a cylinder?

Ⓐ　　　Ⓑ　　　Ⓒ　　　Ⓓ

12. Which figure has four line segments and parallel line segments?

Ⓐ　　　Ⓑ　　　Ⓒ　　　Ⓓ

13. Which picture shows a congruent figure that has been flipped?

Ⓐ　　　Ⓑ　　　Ⓒ　　　Ⓓ

GO ON

14. A line of symmetry is

Ⓐ a figure that has the same size and shape.

Ⓑ a line that divides a figure equally so both sides are exactly alike.

Ⓒ a four-sided figure.

Ⓓ the distance around a figure.

15. If the perimeter of this shape equals 10 inches, how long is the missing side?

3 in.

2 in. ▢ ?

3 in.

Ⓐ 2 in.　　Ⓑ 3 in.

Ⓒ 4 in.　　Ⓓ 5 in.

16. Which shape has an area of 15 square cm?

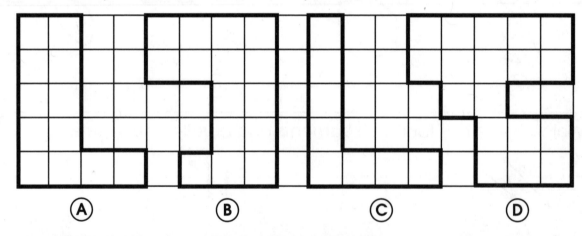

Ⓐ　　　Ⓑ　　　Ⓒ　　　Ⓓ

17. The volume of a figure is

Ⓐ the distance around the figure.

Ⓑ the number of square units it takes to cover the figure.

Ⓒ the number of cubes it takes to fill the figure.

Ⓓ a closed curve.

GO ON

18. Which is true about the pattern?

(A) A circle is always in a triangle.

(B) A star is always in a triangle.

(C) A rectangle is always first.

(D) A big triangle is always next to a rectangle.

19. Which set of figures has the same shape, but a different size?

(A) (B) (C) (D)

20. Find the perimeter of the figure.

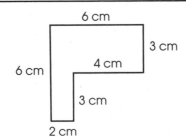

(A) 26 cm   (B) 20 cm

(C) 24 cm   (D) 18 cm

Draw a repeating pattern that includes a closed curve shape and a shape with parallel lines.

STOP

Name

Adding 4-digit numbers without regrouping

Unit 4

To find the sum (answer to an addition problem) of numbers written horizontally, follow these steps:

1. Rewrite the problem vertically, taking care to line up the place value columns.
2. Starting in the ones column, find the sum, and record it in the ones columns.
3. Move to the tens, then the hundreds, and then the thousands, working in that order.

Rewrite the problems vertically, then find the sums.

A. $206 + 3,413 =$

$$
\begin{array}{r}
206 \\
+\,3{,}413 \\
\hline
3{,}619 \\
\end{array}
$$

B. $4,337 + 1,461 =$

C. $2,904 + 3,082 =$

D. $7,321 + 476 =$

E. $902 + 6,093 =$

F. $2,374 + 2,315 =$

G. $8,006 + 942 =$

H. $5,425 + 2,361 =$

Adding with regrouping

Unit 4

When the answer in the ones column is greater than 9, you must regroup. It looks like this:

1. Add the ones.
   Regroup if needed.

$$\begin{array}{r} 1 \\ 3\,|\,8 \\ +\;\;2\,|\,4 \\ \hline |\,2 \end{array}$$

8 + 4 = 12 ones
or 1 ten 2 ones

2. Now add the tens column.

$$\begin{array}{r} 1 \\ 3\,|\,8 \\ +\;\;2\,|\,4 \\ \hline 6\,|\,2 \end{array}$$

Find the sums by regrouping from the ones column to the tens column.

A. $\begin{array}{r} 57 \\ +\;28 \\ \hline \end{array}$ B. $\begin{array}{r} 36 \\ +\;46 \\ \hline \end{array}$ C. $\begin{array}{r} 73 \\ +\;17 \\ \hline \end{array}$ D. $\begin{array}{r} 39 \\ +\;29 \\ \hline \end{array}$ E. $\begin{array}{r} 14 \\ +\;17 \\ \hline \end{array}$ F. $\begin{array}{r} 35 \\ +\;15 \\ \hline \end{array}$

When the sum in the tens column is greater than 9, regroup to the hundreds column. It looks like this:

1. Add the ones.
   Regroup if needed.

$$\begin{array}{r} 172 \\ +\;473 \\ \hline 5 \end{array}$$

2. Add the tens.
   Regroup if needed.

$$\begin{array}{r} 1 \\ 172 \\ +\;473 \\ \hline 45 \end{array}$$

3. Add the hundreds.

$$\begin{array}{r} 1 \\ 172 \\ +\;473 \\ \hline 645 \end{array}$$

Find the sums by regrouping from the tens column to the hundreds column.

G. $\begin{array}{r} 364 \\ +\;271 \\ \hline \end{array}$ H. $\begin{array}{r} 591 \\ +\;186 \\ \hline \end{array}$ I. $\begin{array}{r} 869 \\ +\;\;80 \\ \hline \end{array}$ J. $\begin{array}{r} 453 \\ +\;364 \\ \hline \end{array}$ K. $\begin{array}{r} 272 \\ +\;\;96 \\ \hline \end{array}$

When the sum in the hundreds column is greater than 9, regroup to the thousands. It looks like this:

1. Add the ones.
   Regroup if needed.

$$\begin{array}{r} 4{,}671 \\ +\;824 \\ \hline 5 \end{array}$$

2. Add the tens.
   Regroup if needed.

$$\begin{array}{r} 4{,}671 \\ +\;824 \\ \hline 95 \end{array}$$

3. Add the hundreds.
   Regroup if needed.

$$\begin{array}{r} 1 \\ 4{,}671 \\ +\;824 \\ \hline 495 \end{array}$$

4. Add the thousands.

$$\begin{array}{r} 1 \\ 4{,}671 \\ +\;824 \\ \hline 5{,}495 \end{array}$$

Find the sums by regrouping from the hundreds column to the thousands column.

L. $\begin{array}{r} 3{,}721 \\ +\;1{,}455 \\ \hline \end{array}$ M. $\begin{array}{r} 2{,}504 \\ +\;\;\;712 \\ \hline \end{array}$ N. $\begin{array}{r} 6{,}905 \\ +\;\;\;492 \\ \hline \end{array}$ O. $\begin{array}{r} 863 \\ +\;914 \\ \hline \end{array}$

Adding with multiple regrouping

Some addition problems will require regrouping more than once. Treat each part of the problem as you have practiced to find the sum. Check this out:

1. Add the ones. Regroup if needed.	2. Add the tens. Regroup if needed.	3. Add the hundreds. Regroup if needed.	4. Add the thousands.
1 2,864 + 657 ――――― 1	1 1 2,864 + 657 ――――― 21	1 1 1 2,864 + 657 ――――― 521	1 1 1 2,864 + 657 ――――― 3,521

Find each sum by regrouping. Use the answers to crack the code and answer the riddle.

Who drives away all of his customers?

$$\begin{array}{r} 962 \\ +141 \\ \hline 1,10? \end{array}$$

_____   _____ _____ _____ _____ _____ _____ _____
1,200   1,211 1,200 820 1,371 4,053 1,200 608

_____ _____ _____ _____ _____ _____ !
1,156 631 1,371 1,080 3,107 631

954 + 417 **I**	295 **R** + 336	419 **T** + 792	534 **S** + 958
863 **A** + 337	470 **L** + 188	2,428 **E** + 679	737 **D** + 419
289 **F** + 735	1,566 **C** + 2,487	751 **X** + 69	825 **P** + 208
139 **B** + 469	449 **N** + 154	372 **V** + 708	608 **M** + 98

Name

Adding several numbers

To find the sum of several numbers, use the same steps as before:

1. Add the ones column. Regroup if necessary.
2. Add the tens column. Regroup if necessary.
3. Add the hundreds column. Regroup if necessary.
4. Add the thousands column.

When a problem includes money symbols, do not forget to include the decimal point and dollar sign in your answer.

Who has the wealthiest kingdom? Find each sum. Be sure to include the money symbols in your answers. Then color the answers on the castles. The first castle to be completely colored is located in the most wealthy kingdom!

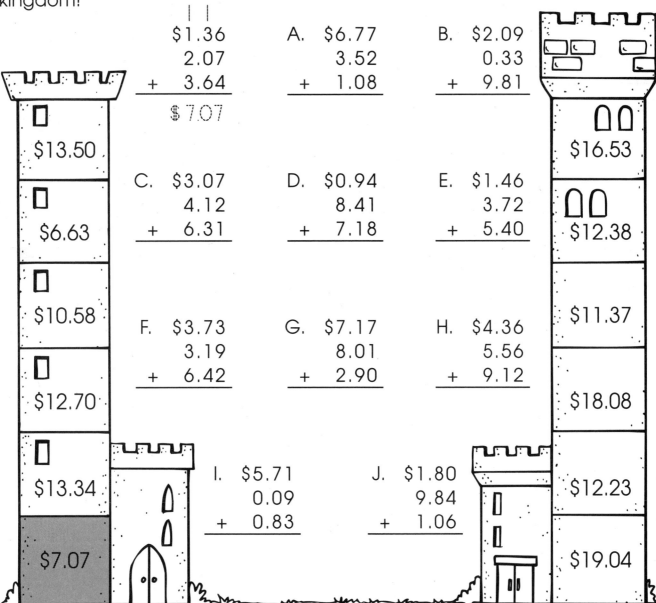

```
   | |
   $1.36        A.  $6.77       B.  $2.09
    2.07            3.52            0.33
 +  3.64        +   1.08       +   9.81
 ─────────      ──────────     ──────────
   $7.07


   C.  $3.07     D.  $0.94       E.  $1.46
       4.12          8.41            3.72
   +   6.31      +   7.18       +   5.40
   ──────────    ──────────     ──────────


   F.  $3.73     G.  $7.17       H.  $4.36
       3.19          8.01            5.56
   +   6.42      +   2.90       +   9.12
   ──────────    ──────────     ──────────


       I.  $5.71          J.  $1.80
           0.09              9.84
       +   0.83          +   1.06
       ──────────        ──────────
```

Left castle: $13.50, $6.63, $10.58, $12.70, $13.34, $7.07

Right castle: $16.53, $12.38, $11.37, $18.08, $12.23, $19.04

Name

Subtracting 4-digit numbers without regrouping   Unit 4

To find the difference (answer to a subtraction problem) between numbers written horizontally, follow these steps:

1. Rewrite the problem vertically, taking care to line up the place value columns.
2. Starting with the ones column, find the difference, and record it in the ones column.
3. Move to the tens, then the hundreds, and then the thousands, working in that order.

Rewrite the problems vertically and then find the answers, called differences.

A.   8,272 − 7,140 =

$$\begin{array}{r} 8,272 \\ -\ 7,140 \\ \hline \end{array}$$

B.   6,942 − 701 =

C.   9,754 − 2,430 =

D.   8,176 − 4,023 =

E.   1,896 − 541 =

F.   8,457 − 3,236 =

G.   7,894 − 5,654 =

H.   9,985 − 5,632 =

Regrouping readiness

As you learn more about subtraction, you will find problems that require regrouping (borrowing). This picture shows regrouping 1 ten for 10 ones:

T	O
5	3

=

T	O
4	13
5̷	3̷

Regroup to make more ones.

A.

T	O
6	4

B.

T	O
8	0

C.

T	O
1	2

D.

T	O
4	5

E.

T	O
7	8

F.

T	O
9	6

G.

T	O
3	3

This picture shows regrouping 1 hundred for 10 tens:

  =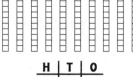

H	T	O
2	4	1

H	T	O
1	14	
2̷	4̷	1

Regroup to make more tens.

H.

H	T	O
1	5	6

I.

H	T	O
7	1	3

J.

H	T	O
9	7	2

K.

H	T	O
5	0	3

This shows regrouping
1 thousand for 10 hundreds:

Th	H	T	O
3	13		
4̷	3̷	6	2

Regroup to make more hundreds.

L.

Th	H	T	O
5	0	3	7

M.

Th	H	T	O
8	4	5	1

N.

Th	H	T	O
9	1	2	6

Subtracting with regrouping

If the top number in the ones column is smaller than the bottom number in the ones column, you must regroup (borrow). It looks like this:

1. Subtract the ones. Regroup if needed.

$$
\begin{array}{r}
\overset{6\ 16}{\cancel{7\ 6}} \\
-\ 3\ 8 \\
\hline
8
\end{array}
$$

7 tens 6 ones =
6 tens 16 ones

2. Subtract the tens.

$$
\begin{array}{r}
\overset{6\ 16}{\cancel{7\ 6}} \\
-\ 3\ 8 \\
\hline
3\ 8
\end{array}
$$

Find the differences by regrouping from the tens column.

A. 92	B. 80	C. 46	D. 37	E. 64	F. 51
− 66	− 14	− 28	− 19	− 8	− 24

When the top number in the tens column is less than the bottom number, you must regroup from the hundreds. It looks like this:

1. Subtract the ones. Regroup if needed.

$$
\begin{array}{r}
6\ 0\ 7 \\
-\ 2\ 8\ 4 \\
\hline
3
\end{array}
$$

2. Subtract the tens. Regroup if needed.

$$
\begin{array}{r}
\overset{5\ 10}{\cancel{6\ 0}\ 7} \\
-\ 2\ 8\ 4 \\
\hline
2\ 3
\end{array}
$$

3. Subtract the hundreds.

$$
\begin{array}{r}
\overset{5\ 10}{\cancel{6\ 0}\ 7} \\
-\ 2\ 8\ 4 \\
\hline
3\ 2\ 3
\end{array}
$$

Find the differences by regrouping from the hundreds column.

G. 918	H. 427	I. 762	J. 586	K. 814
− 176	− 95	− 290	− 192	− 483

When the top number in the hundreds column is smaller than the bottom number, you must regroup from the thousands. It looks like this:

1. Subtract the ones. Regroup if needed.

$$
\begin{array}{r}
7,185 \\
-\ 2,951 \\
\hline
4
\end{array}
$$

2. Subtract the tens. Regroup if needed.

$$
\begin{array}{r}
7,185 \\
-\ 2,951 \\
\hline
34
\end{array}
$$

3. Subtract the hundreds. Regroup if needed.

$$
\begin{array}{r}
\overset{6\ 11}{\cancel{7,1}85} \\
-\ 2,951 \\
\hline
234
\end{array}
$$

4. Subtract the thousands.

$$
\begin{array}{r}
\overset{6\ 11}{\cancel{7,1}85} \\
-\ 2,951 \\
\hline
4,234
\end{array}
$$

Find the differences by regrouping from the thousands column.

L. 3,476	M. 2,380	N. 7,545	O. 6,819
− 1,703	− 600	− 1,832	− 906

Name

Subtracting with multiple regrouping

There will be times that you must regroup more than once in order to subtract. Check this out:

1. 6 10 3,2⁄7⁄0 − 784 ‾‾‾‾‾‾ 6	2. 16 1 6⁄10 3,2⁄7⁄0 − 784 ‾‾‾‾‾‾ 86	3. 11 16 2 1⁄6⁄10 3⁄,2⁄7⁄0 − 784 ‾‾‾‾‾‾ 486	4. 11 16 2 1⁄6⁄10 3⁄,2⁄7⁄0 − 784 ‾‾‾‾‾‾ 2,486

Find the differences.

    | |
   5⁄ | |
  3,6⁄2⁄1⁄
− 1,283
‾‾‾‾‾‾
  2,338

A.   4,197
 −   468
‾‾‾‾‾‾

B.   2,479
 −   890
‾‾‾‾‾‾

C.   5,076
 − 1,256
‾‾‾‾‾‾

D.   9,616
 −   758
‾‾‾‾‾‾

E.   3,804
 − 1,192
‾‾‾‾‾‾

F.   8,941
 −   173
‾‾‾‾‾‾

G.   982
 − 497
‾‾‾‾‾‾

H.   8,263
 − 4,458
‾‾‾‾‾‾

I.   7,603
 −   215
‾‾‾‾‾‾

J.   9,550
 − 4,229
‾‾‾‾‾‾

K.   645
 − 187
‾‾‾‾‾‾

L.   850
 −   76
‾‾‾‾‾‾

M.   2,972
 −   493
‾‾‾‾‾‾

Write your own subtraction problem that uses regrouping two times.

Calculating sums and differences   Unit 4

Remember that regrouping looks different when you add compared to when you subtract.
Watch for the symbols (+, −) that tell you which operation to use.

Find the sums and differences. Then complete the puzzle.

ACROSS

```
1.    1,472          3.    1,853
    -   746              +   927


4.     790           6.     254
    + 631                + 259


8.   7,632           9.   9,216
    -   579              - 8,608


10.  3,657          12.    986
    +   759              - 798
```

DOWN

```
2.     352           5.     728           7.     172
    + 269                - 463               + 178


8.   1,435          11.   3,219          12.   5,189
    -   651              + 3,549             - 3,645
```

Name

Estimating sums and differences

To estimate the answer to an addition or subtraction problem, first round both numbers, then add or subtract. Be sure to read the directions for estimating to the nearest ten or hundred!

Round to the nearest ten to find the estimated answers.

$$
\begin{array}{r}
672 \rightarrow \ 670 \\
- \ 489 \rightarrow -490 \\
\hline
180
\end{array}
$$

A.
$$
\begin{array}{r}
312 \rightarrow \\
+ \ 899 \rightarrow +
\end{array}
$$

B.
$$
\begin{array}{r}
362 \rightarrow \\
- \ 138 \rightarrow -
\end{array}
$$

C.
$$
\begin{array}{r}
841 \rightarrow \\
+ \ 256 \rightarrow +
\end{array}
$$

D.
$$
\begin{array}{r}
918 \rightarrow \\
- \ 466 \rightarrow -
\end{array}
$$

E.
$$
\begin{array}{r}
648 \rightarrow \\
+ \ 214 \rightarrow -
\end{array}
$$

$$
\begin{array}{r}
588 \rightarrow \ 590 \\
- \ 242 \rightarrow -240 \\
\hline
350
\end{array}
$$

Round to the nearest hundred to find the estimated answers.

$$
\begin{array}{r}
689 \rightarrow \ 700 \\
+ \ 413 \rightarrow +400 \\
\hline
1100
\end{array}
$$

F.
$$
\begin{array}{r}
526 \rightarrow \\
+ \ 738 \rightarrow +
\end{array}
$$

G.
$$
\begin{array}{r}
392 \rightarrow \\
- \ 189 \rightarrow -
\end{array}
$$

H.
$$
\begin{array}{r}
165 \rightarrow \\
+ \ 751 \rightarrow +
\end{array}
$$

I.
$$
\begin{array}{r}
948 \rightarrow \\
- \ 299 \rightarrow -
\end{array}
$$

J.
$$
\begin{array}{r}
843 \rightarrow \\
- \ 672 \rightarrow -
\end{array}
$$

Name

Read or listen to the question. Use an extra piece of paper to solve the problems. Fill in the circle beside the best answer.

☐ Example:

673 + 176 =

(A) 849   749

(B) 839   NG (Not Given)

Answer: A

Now try these. You have 20 minutes.

Continue until you see ⬡STOP.

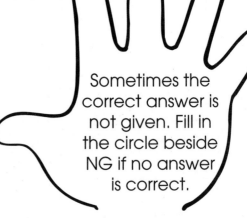

Sometimes the correct answer is not given. Fill in the circle beside NG if no answer is correct.

1.	209 + 2,480 =	2,708 (A)	2,689 (B)	2,698 (C)	2,699 (D)
2.	456 + 473	829 (A)	939 (B)	929 (C)	919 (D)
3.	826 + 195	1,032 (A)	921 (B)	901 (C)	1,021 (D)
4.	$8.34 2.09 + 0.74	$11.17 (A)	$11.07 (B)	$10.17 (C)	NG (D)

GO ON ▷

5. 5,572 − 1,341 =

4,231	3,241	4,831	6,913
A	B	C	D

6. Which shows regrouping to make more tens?

H	T	O
	6	2
9	̸7	̸3

A

H	T	O
8	17	
̸9	̸7	3

B

H	T	O
8	6	
̸9	̸7	3

C

H	T	O
	8	13
9	̸7	̸3

D

7.
```
  608
- 493
```

295	115	125	NG
A	B	C	D

8.
```
  762
- 489
```

273	327	383	358
A	B	C	D

9. Estimate the answer by rounding to the nearest ten.

```
  986
- 442
```

530	540	550	560
A	B	C	D

10.
```
  6,318
+   846
```

5,472	6,154	7,154	7,164
A	B	C	D

11. 5,417 + 3,562 =

8,879	8,989	8,155	NG
A	B	C	D

GO ON

12.

$$3{,}671 \\ +\ 4{,}718$$

8,389 Ⓐ   7,389 Ⓑ   7,289 Ⓒ   NG Ⓓ

13.

$$737 \\ +\ 483$$

1,110 Ⓐ   1,220 Ⓑ   1,120 Ⓒ   1,130 Ⓓ

14.

$$\$5.62 \\ 4.93 \\ +\ 1.28$$

$10.73 Ⓐ $11.73 Ⓑ $11.83 Ⓒ $10.83 Ⓓ

15.   983 – 450 =

533 Ⓐ   633 Ⓑ   543 Ⓒ   643 Ⓓ

16. Which problem shows the correct way to regroup?

$$\overset{6\ 4}{6{,}3\cancel{7}\cancel{5}} \\ -\ 1{,}762$$

$$\overset{5\ 13}{\cancel{6}{,}375} \\ -\ 1{,}762$$

$$\overset{12\ 6}{6{,}\cancel{3}75} \\ -\ 1{,}762$$

NG

Ⓐ   Ⓑ   Ⓒ   Ⓓ

17.

$$7{,}392 \\ -\ 1{,}480$$

6,112 Ⓐ   6,012 Ⓑ   5,812 Ⓒ   5,912 Ⓓ

GO ON

18.
$$\begin{array}{r} 9{,}354 \\ -\ 2{,}693 \end{array}$$

7,341 Ⓐ

6,661 Ⓑ

6,641 Ⓒ

7,661 Ⓓ

19. Estimate the answer by rounding to the nearest hundred.

$$\begin{array}{r} 890 \\ -\ 463 \end{array}$$

200 Ⓐ

300 Ⓑ

400 Ⓒ

500 Ⓓ

20. Which problem shows regrouping correctly to make more ones and hundreds?

3 16 8 11
4,69X
− 2,736

Ⓐ

3 15 18 11
4,69X
− 2,736

Ⓑ

3 16 8 10
4,69X
− 2,736

Ⓒ

3 15   11
4,69X
− 2,736

Ⓓ

Write an addition problem that requires regrouping two times.

STOP

Midway Review Test Name Grid

Write your name in pencil in the boxes along the top. Begin with your last name. Fill in as many letters as will fit. Then follow the columns straight down and bubble in the letters that correspond with the letters in your name. Complete the rest of the information the same way. You may use a piece of scrap paper to help you keep your place.

STUDENT'S NAME			
LAST		FIRST	MI

Name grid columns (bubbles A–Z for each letter column)

SCHOOL
TEACHER
FEMALE ○　　　MALE ○

DATE OF BIRTH

MONTH	DAY		YEAR	
JAN ○	⓪	⓪	⓪	⓪
FEB ○	①	①	①	①
MAR ○	②	②	②	②
APR ○	③	③	③	③
MAY ○		④	④	④
JUN ○		⑤	⑤	⑤
JUL ○		⑥	⑥	⑥
AUG ○		⑦	⑦	⑦
SEP ○		⑧	⑧	⑧
OCT ○		⑨	⑨	⑨
NOV ○				
DEC ○				

GRADE　③　④　⑤

Midway Review Test Answer Sheet

Pay close attention when transferring your answers. Fill in the bubbles neatly and completely. You may use a piece of scrap paper to help you keep your place.

SAMPLES
A Ⓐ Ⓑ ● Ⓓ
B Ⓕ ● Ⓗ Ⓙ

1 Ⓐ Ⓑ Ⓒ Ⓓ
2 Ⓕ Ⓖ Ⓗ Ⓙ
3 Ⓐ Ⓑ Ⓒ Ⓓ
4 Ⓕ Ⓖ Ⓗ Ⓙ
5 Ⓐ Ⓑ Ⓒ Ⓓ
6 Ⓕ Ⓖ Ⓗ Ⓙ

7 Ⓐ Ⓑ Ⓒ Ⓓ
8 Ⓕ Ⓖ Ⓗ Ⓙ
9 Ⓐ Ⓑ Ⓒ Ⓓ
10 Ⓕ Ⓖ Ⓗ Ⓙ
11 Ⓐ Ⓑ Ⓒ Ⓓ
12 Ⓕ Ⓖ Ⓗ Ⓙ

13 Ⓐ Ⓑ Ⓒ Ⓓ
14 Ⓕ Ⓖ Ⓗ Ⓙ
15 Ⓐ Ⓑ Ⓒ Ⓓ
16 Ⓕ Ⓖ Ⓗ Ⓙ
17 Ⓐ Ⓑ Ⓒ Ⓓ
18 Ⓕ Ⓖ Ⓗ Ⓙ

19 Ⓐ Ⓑ Ⓒ Ⓓ
20 Ⓕ Ⓖ Ⓗ Ⓙ

Name

Read or listen to the question. Use an extra piece of paper to solve the problems and to keep your place on the score sheet. Fill in the circle beside the best answer completely and neatly.

Remember your Helping Hand Strategies:

1. Read all of the choices before you answer.

☐ Example:

Find the sum.
```
    362
+    38
```

2. When you are unsure, cross out the answers you know are incorrect and make your best guess from those that are left.

390   500   400   410
Ⓐ   Ⓑ   Ⓒ   Ⓓ

Answer: C because you must regroup to the tens and hundreds column.

3. With picture answers, cover some of the choices so you see only one picture at a time.

Now try these. You have 25 minutes.

Continue until you see ⟨STOP⟩.

4. Sometimes the correct answer is not given. Fill in the circle beside NG if no answer is correct.

---

1. Which number shows a 7 in the tens place and a 6 in the thousands place?

6,742   6,472   7,642   7,462
Ⓐ   Ⓑ   Ⓒ   Ⓓ

---

2. Janie's swim class starts at 8:15. It lasts 1 ½ hours. What time will Janie's class end?

Ⓕ   Ⓖ   Ⓗ   Ⓙ

GO ON ▷

Name _____

3. What shape is the object?

(A) pyramid   (B) cube

(C) cylinder   (D) rectangular prism

4.
```
  382
  106
+ 470
```

848 (F)   948 (G)   958 (H)   968 (J)

5. 46 − 28 =

22 (A)   12 (B)   28 (C)   18 (D)

6. Which of the following shows 3,492 in expanded form?

(F) 3,000 + 400 + 90 + 2   (G) 300 + 4,000 + 90 + 2

(H) 30 + 4 + 9,000 + 200   (J) 3,000 + 40 + 900 + 2

7. Which box shows three even numbers?

6 3 5 4 8	1 4 9 5 2	7 3 1 0 2	3 9 2 6 1
(A)	(B)	(C)	(D)

GO ON →

8. Which shows figures that are not congruent?

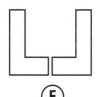   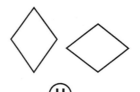

Ⓕ   Ⓖ   Ⓗ   Ⓙ

9.   56 + 29 =

74   85   75   NG
Ⓐ   Ⓑ   Ⓒ   Ⓓ

10. Round the problem to the nearest hundred to estimate the difference.

856
− 193

800   600   900   700
Ⓕ   Ⓖ   Ⓗ   Ⓙ

11. How many tens are in 9,328?

9   3   2   8
Ⓐ   Ⓑ   Ⓒ   Ⓓ

12. Which number is four hundred eighty-one?

418   481   841   801
Ⓕ   Ⓖ   Ⓗ   Ⓙ

13. Which figure has an area of 10 square units?

Ⓐ   Ⓑ   Ⓒ   Ⓓ

GO ON ▷

14.   862
        + 349

1,110 (F)   1,220 (G)   1,120 (H)   NG (J)

15.   4,731
        − 1,815

3,926 (A)   3,124 (B)   2,916 (C)   NG (D)

16. Which group of numbers shows counting by threes?

30, 35, 40 (F)   42, 45, 48 (G)   43, 44, 45 (H)   13, 23, 33 (J)

17. What time does the clock show?

(A) quarter past 6:00

(B) quarter till 9:00

(C) half past 9:00

(D) quarter till 7:00

18. Which figure shows a line of symmetry?

(F)   (G)   (H)   (J)

19. What are the next three numbers in this pattern?

18, 22, 26, ___, ___, ___

27, 28, 29 (A)   30, 34, 38 (B)   32, 36, 40 (C)   29, 32, 35 (D)

GO ON

Midway Review Test

20. Which greater than/less than statement is not true?

629 > 619	3,103 < 4,031	946 > 970	6,017 < 6,936
Ⓕ	Ⓖ	Ⓗ	Ⓙ

Write two numbers that match all of these clues.

1. One number is even, and the other number is odd.
2. Both numbers are 3-digit numbers.
3. One number is less than 310.
4. Their sum equals 765.

STOP

Name _____

To **multiply** means to use repeated addition. It is more easily understood if you can imagine making equal groups, then adding all of the groups together. It looks like this:

The answer to a multiplication problem is called the product. The numbers being multiplied are called factors.

● ● ● ●   4 + 4 + 4
● ● ● ●   3 groups of 4
● ● ● ●   3 x 4 ← factors
            12 ← product

Write an addition and multiplication problem for each picture. Then find the sum and the product.

A.

X X X X X
X X X X X
X X X X X

□ + □ + □ = □

□ x □ = □

B.

☆ ☆ ☆
☆ ☆ ☆

□ + □ = □

□ x □ = □

C.

O O
O O
O O
O O

□ + □ + □ + □ = □

□ x □ = □

D.

℃ ℃ ℃ ℃
℃ ℃ ℃ ℃

□ + □ = □

□ x □ = □

E.

X X X
X X X
X X X

□ + □ + □ = □

□ x □ = □

F.

☆ ☆ ☆ ☆
☆ ☆ ☆ ☆
☆ ☆ ☆ ☆

□ + □ + □ = □

□ x □ = □

G.

O O
O O
O O

□ + □ + □ = □

□ x □ = □

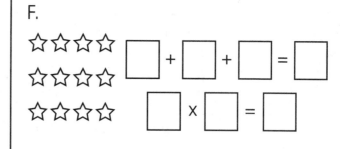

H.

℃ ℃ ℃ ℃ ℃
℃ ℃ ℃ ℃ ℃

□ + □ = □

□ x □ = □

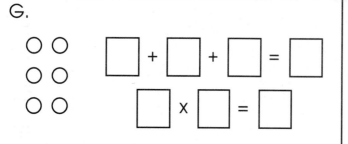

Name

Learning basic multiplication facts

Like addition and subtraction, there are basic multiplication problems that you will want to memorize. These basic facts will help you multiply bigger numbers later. Use this list of helpful hints as you begin to memorize the basic facts.

Read each helpful hint. Find the products as you move through the list.

☐ x 0	Always equals 0!	$5 \times 0 = $ ☐ $0 \times 0 = $ ☐ $0 \times 2 = $ ☐ $0 \times 3 = $ ☐
☐ x 1	Always equals the other factor!	$6 \times 1 = $ ☐ $9 \times 1 = $ ☐ $1 \times 7 = $ ☐ $1 \times 2 = $ ☐
☐ x 2	Count by 2 ☐ times! Find 5 x 2: 2 4 6 8 10	$4 \times 2 = $ ☐ $5 \times 2 = $ ☐ $2 \times 3 = $ ☐ $2 \times 4 = $ ☐
☐ x 3	Count by 3 ☐ times! Find 4 x 3: 3 6 9 12 15	$3 \times 3 = $ ☐ $3 \times 2 = $ ☐ $5 \times 3 = $ ☐ $4 \times 3 = $ ☐
☐ x 4	Multiply by 2. Then double the product. Find 3 x 4: $3 \times 2 = 6$ $6 + 6 = 12$	$2 \times 4 = $ ☐ $1 \times 4 = $ ☐ $4 \times 4 = $ ☐ $4 \times 6 = $ ☐
☐ x 5	Count by 5 ☐ times! Find 4 x 5: 5 10 15 20 25	$1 \times 5 = $ ☐ $6 \times 5 = $ ☐ $5 \times 3 = $ ☐ $5 \times 8 = $ ☐
☐ x 6	Multiply by 5. Multiply by 1. Add the products. Find 7 x 6: $7 \times 5 = 35$ $7 \times 1 = 7$ $35 + 7 = 42$	$2 \times 6 = $ ☐ $6 \times 7 = $ ☐ $6 \times 4 = $ ☐ $6 \times 3 = $ ☐
☐ x 7	You know a helpful hint for the other factor. The only new problems will be $7 \times 7 = 49$ and $7 \times 8 = 56$.	$7 \times 2 = $ ☐ $7 \times 8 = $ ☐ $7 \times 5 = $ ☐ $6 \times 7 = $ ☐
☐ x 8	You know a helpful hint for the other factor. The only new problem will be $8 \times 8 = 64$.	$3 \times 8 = $ ☐ $5 \times 8 = $ ☐ $6 \times 8 = $ ☐ $8 \times 8 = $ ☐
☐ x 9	The tens digit of the answer is always 1 less than the first factor. Then the sum of the tens and ones digits will always equal 9.	$3 \times 9 = $ ☐ $9 \times 6 = $ ☐ $7 \times 9 = $ ☐ $9 \times 9 = $ ☐

Name

Practicing basic multiplication facts

Unit 5

Remember the helpful hints as you begin to memorize the basic facts.

Find the products.

A. 6 x 4 = _____   2 x 3 = _____   8 x 3 = _____   8 x 8 = _____

B. 8 x 6 = _____   9 x 7 = _____   5 x 9 = _____   9 x 1 = _____

C. 5 x 3 = _____   7 x 4 = _____   8 x 2 = _____   9 x 8 = _____

D. 6 x 6 = _____   3 x 7 = _____   5 x 5 = _____   4 x 3 = _____

E. 9 x 2 = _____   8 x 7 = _____   1 x 10 = _____   6 x 9 = _____

F.   4   4   9   6
   x 8   x 4   x 3   x 2

G.   7   9   7   5
   x 7   x 9   x 2   x 4

H.   6   5   2   7
   x 5   x 8   x 5   x 5

I.   9   6   3   2
   x 4   x 3   x 3   x 2

Finding the facts

Unit 5

Remember to use the helpful hints to help you memorize the basic facts.

Find the products for the factors below. Then use the code to answer the riddles.

A	B	C	D	E	F	G	H	I	J	K	L	M	N	O	P	Q	R	S	T	U	V	W	X	Y	Z
64	4	42	7	24	16	0	18	40	11	19	49	59	25	12	13	21	56	8	54	32	28	45	60	9	14

What can you hold in your left hand but not in your right hand?

—— —— —— ——
3 x 3   6 x 2   8 x 4   7 x 8

—— —— —— —— ——
8 x 7   5 x 8   1 x 0   6 x 3   6 x 9

—— —— —— —— —— !
8 x 3   7 x 7   2 x 2   3 x 4   9 x 5

Why is it so easy to weigh fish?

—— —— —— —— —— —— ——
4 x 1   6 x 4   6 x 7   8 x 8   4 x 8   2 x 4   3 x 8

—— —— —— ——   —— —— —— ——
4 x 4   8 x 5   1 x 8   9 x 2   3 x 6   8 x 8   7 x 4   4 x 6

—— —— —— —— ——   —— —— ——
9 x 6   2 x 9   8 x 3   5 x 8   7 x 8   3 x 4   9 x 5   5 x 5

—— —— —— —— —— —— !
4 x 2   7 x 6   8 x 8   7 x 7   6 x 4   8 x 1

Name

Multiplying with a 2-digit factor (no regrouping)

Follow these steps to multiply with a 2-digit factor.

1. Multiply the ones.

```
  3 2
x   4
-----
    8
```

2. Multiply the bottom factor in the ones column with the top factor in the tens column.

```
  3 2
x   4
-----
1 2 8
```

Find the products.

```
    9 4
x     2
-------
  1 8 8
```

```
A.   6 3
   x   3
   -----
```

```
B.   8 0
   x   8
   -----
```

```
C.   4 2
   x   3
   -----
```

```
D.   6 1
   x   9
   -----
```

```
E.   7 2
   x   2
   -----
```

```
F.   9 1
   x   7
   -----
```

```
G.   5 2
   x   4
   -----
```

```
H.   7 3
   x   3
   -----
```

```
I.   6 0
   x   6
   -----
```

```
J.   5 3
   x   2
   -----
```

```
K.   7 1
   x   5
   -----
```

```
L.   9 2
   x   4
   -----
```

```
M.   2 1
   x   9
   -----
```

```
N.   9 1
   x   8
   -----
```

```
O.   8 2
   x   2
   -----
```

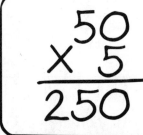

```
  5 0
x   5
-----
2 5 0
```

Teach & Test Math: Grade 3

Name

Multiplying with regrouping   Unit 5

Remember regrouping? There will be times that we must regroup when we multiply.
Check this out:

1. Multiply the ones. Regroup if needed.

$$\begin{array}{r} 3 \\ 5\,6 \\ \times \quad 5 \\ \hline 0 \end{array}$$

2. Multiply the tens. Add the extra tens.

$$\begin{array}{r} 3 \\ 5\,6 \\ \times \quad 5 \\ \hline 2\,8\,0 \end{array}$$

Find the products.

$$\begin{array}{r} 99 \\ \times \quad 2 \\ \hline 198 \end{array}$$

A. $\begin{array}{r} 67 \\ \times \quad 5 \\ \hline \end{array}$

B. $\begin{array}{r} 74 \\ \times \quad 4 \\ \hline \end{array}$

C. $\begin{array}{r} 58 \\ \times \quad 7 \\ \hline \end{array}$

D. $\begin{array}{r} 64 \\ \times \quad 9 \\ \hline \end{array}$

E. $\begin{array}{r} 57 \\ \times \quad 3 \\ \hline \end{array}$

F. $\begin{array}{r} 25 \\ \times \quad 6 \\ \hline \end{array}$

G. $\begin{array}{r} 62 \\ \times \quad 8 \\ \hline \end{array}$

H. $\begin{array}{r} 56 \\ \times \quad 8 \\ \hline \end{array}$

I. $\begin{array}{r} 35 \\ \times \quad 7 \\ \hline \end{array}$

J. $\begin{array}{r} 23 \\ \times \quad 9 \\ \hline \end{array}$

K. $\begin{array}{r} 83 \\ \times \quad 6 \\ \hline \end{array}$

L. $\begin{array}{r} 94 \\ \times \quad 9 \\ \hline \end{array}$

M. $\begin{array}{r} 76 \\ \times \quad 6 \\ \hline \end{array}$

N. $\begin{array}{r} 82 \\ \times \quad 8 \\ \hline \end{array}$

Write a multiplication problem that shows regrouping in the ones place.

Name

Multiplying with regrouping

To multiply with a 3-digit factor, follow these steps:

1. Multiply the ones. Regroup if needed.

$$\begin{array}{r} 2 \\ 265 \\ \times\ \ 5 \\ \hline 5 \end{array}$$

2. Multiply the tens. Add the extra tens. Regroup if needed.

$$\begin{array}{r} 32 \\ 265 \\ \times\ \ 5 \\ \hline 25 \end{array}$$

3. Multiply the hundreds. Add the extra hundreds.

$$\begin{array}{r} 32 \\ 265 \\ \times\ \ 5 \\ \hline 1325 \end{array}$$

Find the products.

$$\begin{array}{r} | \\ 364 \\ \times\ \ 2 \\ \hline 728 \end{array}$$

A.
$$\begin{array}{r} 378 \\ \times\ \ 2 \\ \hline \end{array}$$

B.
$$\begin{array}{r} 354 \\ \times\ \ 3 \\ \hline \end{array}$$

C.
$$\begin{array}{r} 671 \\ \times\ \ 4 \\ \hline \end{array}$$

D.
$$\begin{array}{r} 500 \\ \times\ \ 3 \\ \hline \end{array}$$

E.
$$\begin{array}{r} 534 \\ \times\ \ 8 \\ \hline \end{array}$$

F.
$$\begin{array}{r} 439 \\ \times\ \ 2 \\ \hline \end{array}$$

G.
$$\begin{array}{r} 266 \\ \times\ \ 5 \\ \hline \end{array}$$

H.
$$\begin{array}{r} 180 \\ \times\ \ 5 \\ \hline \end{array}$$

I.
$$\begin{array}{r} 911 \\ \times\ \ 9 \\ \hline \end{array}$$

J.
$$\begin{array}{r} 236 \\ \times\ \ 3 \\ \hline \end{array}$$

K.
$$\begin{array}{r} 741 \\ \times\ \ 3 \\ \hline \end{array}$$

L.
$$\begin{array}{r} 372 \\ \times\ \ 4 \\ \hline \end{array}$$

M.
$$\begin{array}{r} 407 \\ \times\ \ 2 \\ \hline \end{array}$$

N.
$$\begin{array}{r} 165 \\ \times\ \ 7 \\ \hline \end{array}$$

O.
$$\begin{array}{r} 290 \\ \times\ \ 6 \\ \hline \end{array}$$

Name

Multiplying money

To multiply money, follow the same steps you would use to multiply. When you have completed the problem, be sure to include the dollar sign and decimal.

```
    5 2
  $5.63
x       8
  $45.04
```

```
    5 1
  $1.93
x       6
  $11.58
```

Find the products. Don't forget to include the dollar sign and decimal.

A. $7.30
   x   5

B. $3.41
   x   8

C. $8.24
   x   3

D. $6.15
   x   7

E. $0.68
   x   2

F. $1.98
   x   4

G. $3.62
   x   6

H. $2.99
   x   5

I. $1.37
   x   7

J. $0.91
   x   9

K. $4.00
   x   6

L. $1.23
   x   9

M. $0.11
   x   8

N. $3.82
   x   3

O. $0.74
   x   4

P. $6.80
   x   7

Name _____

Read or listen to the question. Use an extra piece of paper to solve the problems. Fill in the circle beside the best answer.

☐ Example:

$$\begin{array}{r} 28 \\ \times\ \ 3 \\ \hline \end{array}$$

(A) 64   (B) 24

(C) 86   (D) 84

When using scratch paper, copy carefully.

Answer: D because you must regroup and then add the extra tens.

Now try these. You have 20 minutes. Continue until you see STOP.

---

1. Mark the number sentence that matches the picture.

@ @ @
@ @ @
@ @ @

(A) 3 x 9   (B) 3 x 6

(C) 3 x 3   (D) 3 x 2

---

2. 3 x 5 means the same as

(A) adding 3 and 5   (B) subtracting 3 from 5

(C) counting by five 5 times   (D) counting by five 3 times

---

3. 6 x 5 =

25	30	11	NG
(A)	(B)	(C)	(D)

4.
$$\begin{array}{r} 7 \\ \times\ 7 \\ \hline \end{array}$$

14	77	49	56
(A)	(B)	(C)	(D)

GO ON ▷

Unit 5 Test

5.

$$\begin{array}{r} 61 \\ \times\ \ 3 \\ \hline \end{array}$$

183 Ⓐ 108 Ⓑ 181 Ⓒ 123 Ⓓ

6.

$$\begin{array}{r} 74 \\ \times\ \ 6 \\ \hline \end{array}$$

364 Ⓐ 444 Ⓑ 384 Ⓒ NG Ⓓ

7.

$$\begin{array}{r} 308 \\ \times\ \ 2 \\ \hline \end{array}$$

512 Ⓐ 612 Ⓑ 606 Ⓒ 616 Ⓓ

8.

$$\begin{array}{r} \$2.90 \\ \times\ \ 5 \\ \hline \end{array}$$

$14.50 Ⓐ $10.50 Ⓑ $14.55 Ⓒ NG Ⓓ

9. Which problem has been completed correctly?

$$\begin{array}{r} 65 \\ \times\ \ 3 \\ \hline 195 \end{array}\qquad \begin{array}{r} 65 \\ \times\ \ 3 \\ \hline 1815 \end{array}\qquad \begin{array}{r} 65 \\ \times\ \ 3 \\ \hline 185 \end{array}\qquad \begin{array}{r} 65 \\ \times\ \ 3 \\ \hline 98 \end{array}$$

Ⓐ   Ⓑ   Ⓒ   Ⓓ

10. Mark the sentence that does not match the picture.

☆ ☆ ☆ ☆
☆ ☆ ☆ ☆
☆ ☆ ☆ ☆

Ⓐ 3 groups of 4   Ⓑ 3 x 4

Ⓒ 3 + 3 + 3 + 3   Ⓓ 3 + 4

GO ON

11. $8 \times 8 =$

49	54	64	72
Ⓐ	Ⓑ	Ⓒ	Ⓓ

12.
$$\begin{array}{r} 9 \\ \times\ 4 \\ \hline \end{array}$$

32	36	13	NG
Ⓐ	Ⓑ	Ⓒ	Ⓓ

13. $5 \times 8 =$

35	48	40	45
Ⓐ	Ⓑ	Ⓒ	Ⓓ

14.
$$\begin{array}{r} 90 \\ \times\ 8 \\ \hline \end{array}$$

720	728	810	NG
Ⓐ	Ⓑ	Ⓒ	Ⓓ

15.
$$\begin{array}{r} 68 \\ \times\ 3 \\ \hline \end{array}$$

184	204	136	144
Ⓐ	Ⓑ	Ⓒ	Ⓓ

16.
$$\begin{array}{r} 620 \\ \times\ 9 \\ \hline \end{array}$$

5,480	5,589	5,840	NG
Ⓐ	Ⓑ	Ⓒ	Ⓓ

17.
$$\begin{array}{r} \$4.17 \\ \times\ 8 \\ \hline \end{array}$$

\$33.36	\$33.28	\$32.86	\$25.36
Ⓐ	Ⓑ	Ⓒ	Ⓓ

GO ON

Unit 5 Test

18. $7 \times 3 =$

21   24   28   32
Ⓐ   Ⓑ   Ⓒ   Ⓓ

19. In the problem below, which number is called the product?

$8 \times 6 = 48$

8   6   4   48
Ⓐ   Ⓑ   Ⓒ   Ⓓ

20.

$$\begin{array}{r} 649 \\ \times \quad 3 \\ \hline \end{array}$$

1,882   1,897   1,947   1,942
Ⓐ   Ⓑ   Ⓒ   Ⓓ

Draw a picture to show that $4 \times 7 = 28$. What other math sentences can you draw from the picture?

STOP

Name

Understanding division   Unit 6

To **divide** means to make equal groups or to share equally. The answer to a division problem is called the quotient. It looks like this:

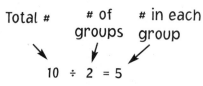

Total #   # of groups   # in each group

$12 \div 3 = 4$

Total #   # of groups   # in each group

$10 \div 2 = 5$

Circle equal groups to find the quotient.

A. ☆ ☆ ☆ ☆ ☆ ☆ ☆ ☆ ☆ ☆ $10 \div 5 = \boxed{}$	B. ▢ ▢ ▢ ▢ ▢ ▢ ▢ ▢ ▢ ▢ ▢ ▢ ▢ ▢ ▢ $15 \div 3 = \boxed{}$	C. ○ ○ ○ ○ ○ ○ $6 \div 3 = \boxed{}$
D. ☺ ☺ ☺ ☺ ☺ ☺ ☺ ☺ $8 \div 2 = \boxed{}$	E. ☆ ☆ ☆ ☆ ☆ ☆ ☆ ☆ ☆ $9 \div 3 = \boxed{}$	F. ▢ ▢ ▢ ▢ ▢ ▢ ▢ ▢ ▢ ▢ ▢ ▢ $12 \div 4 = \boxed{}$
G. ○ ○ ○ ○ ○ ○ ○ ○ ○ ○ ○ ○ $12 \div 6 = \boxed{}$	H. ☺ ☺ ☺ ☺ ☺ ☺ ☺ ☺ ☺ ☺ ☺ ☺ ☺ ☺ ☺ ☺ ☺ ☺ $18 \div 3 = \boxed{}$	I. ☆ ☆ ☆ ☆ ☆ ☆ ☆ ☆ ☆ ☆ ☆ ☆ ☆ ☆ $14 \div 7 = \boxed{}$

Name

Connecting multiplication and division—fact families

Multiplication depends on equal groups, so you can use the multiplication basic facts to help you divide. The two are related, like families. They are called fact families. It looks like this:

3 groups of 4

$3 \times 4 = 12$

12 divided into 4 equal groups

$12 \div 4 = 3$

Use the missing factor to help you find the quotient.

A.
$2 \times \boxed{} = 8$

$8 \div 2 = \boxed{}$

B.
$3 \times \boxed{} = 9$

$9 \div 3 = \boxed{}$

C.
$4 \times \boxed{} = 16$

$16 \div 4 = \boxed{}$

D.
$8 \times \boxed{} = 40$

$40 \div 8 = \boxed{}$

E.
$5 \times \boxed{} = 25$

$25 \div 5 = \boxed{}$

F.
$6 \times \boxed{} = 18$

$18 \div 6 = \boxed{}$

G.
$4 \times \boxed{} = 12$

$12 \div 4 = \boxed{}$

H.
$7 \times \boxed{} = 42$

$42 \div 7 = \boxed{}$

I.
$3 \times \boxed{} = 15$

$15 \div 3 = \boxed{}$

J.
$9 \times \boxed{} = 81$

$81 \div 9 = \boxed{}$

K.
$2 \times \boxed{} = 10$

$10 \div 2 = \boxed{}$

L.
$2 \times \boxed{} = 4$

$4 \div 2 = \boxed{}$

M.
$5 \times \boxed{} = 20$

$20 \div 5 = \boxed{}$

N.
$3 \times \boxed{} = 6$

$6 \div 3 = \boxed{}$

O.
$6 \times \boxed{} = 36$

$36 \div 6 = \boxed{}$

Name

As with multiplication, the basic facts of division will eventually be memorized and used for long division. Watch for these basic facts to be written two ways:

dividend divisor quotient

$12 \div 3 = 4$

divisor   4 ← quotient

$3 \overline{)12}$ ← dividend

Use what you know about multiplication to find the quotients.

$12 \div 6 = \boxed{2}$

$6 \times \boxed{2} = 12$

A. $24 \div 4 = \square$

B. $40 \div 5 = \square$

C. $16 \div 4 = \square$

D. $21 \div 7 = \square$

E. $9 \div 3 = \square$

F. $36 \div 6 = \square$

G. $24 \div 8 = \square$

H. $20 \div 4 = \square$

I. $15 \div 5 = \square$

J. $12 \div 4 = \square$

K. $25 \div 5 = \square$

$9 \overline{)27}^{\ 3}$

L. $9 \overline{)36}$

M. $9 \overline{)81}$

N. $6 \overline{)54}$

O. $9 \overline{)63}$

P. $5 \overline{)45}$

Q. $7 \overline{)56}$

R. $7 \overline{)49}$

S. $8 \overline{)64}$

T. $7 \overline{)42}$

How many basic division facts with a quotient of 6 can you list?

Practicing basic division facts

Unit 6

Remember to use your knowledge of multiplication facts to help you divide.

Did you know the first bicycles had no pedals? People walked them along until they came to a hill. Then they would jump on and ride down the hill. These early bikes were called swift walkers.

In what year did the first bicycles arrive in the U.S.?

They arrived in _____ _____ _____ _____.

Divide. To find the answer to the question, write the quotients in the shoes in order on the blanks above.

$$7\overline{)42} \quad \overset{6}{}$$

A. $9\overline{)9}$

B. $6\overline{)36}$

C. $5\overline{)40}$

D. $8\overline{)48}$

E. $3\overline{)27}$

F.  $8\overline{)64}$

G. $8\overline{)16}$

H. $9\overline{)36}$

I. $7\overline{)49}$

J. $4\overline{)28}$

K. $8\overline{)48}$

L. $7\overline{)63}$

M. $6\overline{)6}$

N. $6\overline{)42}$

O. $6\overline{)36}$

P. $8\overline{)72}$

Q. $8\overline{)32}$

R. $4\overline{)16}$

S. $6\overline{)54}$

T. $4\overline{)36}$

U. $8\overline{)56}$

V. $9\overline{)81}$

W. $7\overline{)49}$

Name

Dividing with place value patterns

You can use the basic facts and patterns to find other quotients like these:

8 ÷ 4 = 2

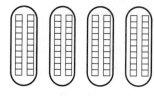

80 ÷ 4 = 20

800 ÷ 4 = 200

Use the basic facts to help you find the quotients.

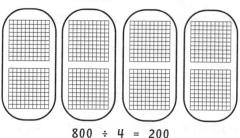

200 ÷ 2 = [100]

A. 350 ÷ 7 = [ ]

B. 720 ÷ 8 = [ ]

C. 400 ÷ 8 = [ ]

D. 810 ÷ 9 = [ ]

E. 630 ÷ 7 = [ ]

F. 210 ÷ 7 = [ ]

G. 420 ÷ 7 = [ ]

H. 540 ÷ 9 = [ ]

I. 360 ÷ 6 = [ ]

250 ÷ 5 = 50

J. 4⟌240

K. 4⟌160

L. 8⟌80

M. 5⟌200

N. 2⟌180

O. 4⟌120

P. 6⟌120

Q. 5⟌250

Name

Dividing with remainders

Sometimes when you try to make equal groups, there are numbers left over. They are called remainders.
Use these steps to find remainders:

Find

$4\overline{)18}$

4 groups of 4 = 16

2 left over = R 2

So . . . $4\overline{)18}$ 4 R2

1. Does 4 x __ = 18

   no!

   Think: 4 x __ is the closest to 18?

2. Use the closest smaller dividend: 4 x 4 = 16

   $$4\overline{)18} \quad \begin{array}{r} 4 \\ \hline 18 \\ 16 \end{array}$$

3. Subtract to find the remainder.

   $$\begin{array}{r} 4\ R2 \\ 4\overline{)18} \\ -\ 16 \\ \hline 2 \end{array}$$

The remainder is always less than the divisor.

Find the quotients and their remainders.

$$\begin{array}{r} 4\ R2 \\ 8\overline{)34} \\ -\ 32 \\ \hline 2 \end{array}$$

A. $4\overline{)26}$

B. $7\overline{)67}$

C. $3\overline{)17}$

D. $9\overline{)29}$

E. $5\overline{)42}$

F. $6\overline{)47}$

G. $9\overline{)83}$

H. $6\overline{)39}$

I. $4\overline{)19}$

J. $5\overline{)24}$

K. $8\overline{)79}$

L. $7\overline{)41}$

M. $6\overline{)23}$

N. $9\overline{)60}$

O. $4\overline{)15}$

Name _____

Dividing with 2-digit numbers (no remainders) Unit 6

Sometimes when you look at a problem, the dividend is much larger than the basic facts you have learned. These problems will require you to do more than one step to find the quotient. Use these steps to help you:

1. Does 4 x __ = 5?

   no!

   $4\overline{)56}$

2. Use the closest smaller dividend:

   4 x 1 = 4

   $\begin{array}{r} 1 \\ 4\overline{)56} \\ \underline{4} \end{array}$

3. Subtract to find the remainder. Bring down the 6.

   $\begin{array}{r} 1 \\ 4\overline{)56} \\ \underline{-4\downarrow} \\ 16 \end{array}$

4. Does 4 x __ = 16? Yes! 4 x 4 = 16

   $\begin{array}{r} 14 \\ 4\overline{)56} \\ \underline{-4} \\ 16 \end{array}$

Find the quotients.

$\begin{array}{r} 16 \\ 6\overline{)96} \\ \underline{-6\downarrow} \\ 36 \end{array}$

A. $2\overline{)98}$

B. $5\overline{)90}$

C. $7\overline{)84}$

D. $5\overline{)75}$

E. $3\overline{)87}$

F. $8\overline{)96}$

G. $2\overline{)76}$

H. $6\overline{)84}$

I. $3\overline{)54}$

J. $4\overline{)96}$

K. $5\overline{)85}$

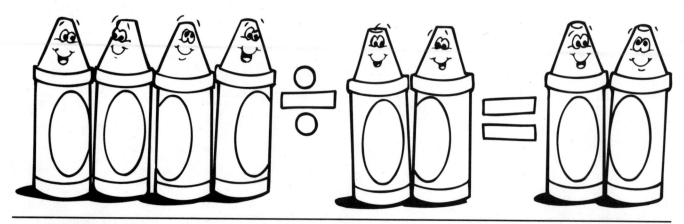

Name

Dividing 2-digit problems with remainders

When numbers can't be divided evenly in a 2-digit number, you may have a remainder. Use these steps to help you:

1. Divide as before.

$6 \times \underline{} = 8$

$$\begin{array}{r} 1 \\ 6\overline{)89} \\ -6 \\ \hline 29 \end{array}$$

2. Use the closest smaller dividend:

$6 \times 4 = 24$

$$\begin{array}{r} 14 \\ 6\overline{)89} \\ -6 \\ \hline 29 \\ -24 \end{array}$$

3. Subtract to find the remainder.

$$\begin{array}{r} 14\ R5 \\ 6\overline{)89} \\ -6 \\ \hline 29 \\ -24 \\ \hline 5 \end{array}$$

Find the quotients and their remainders.

A. $3\overline{)89}$

B. $4\overline{)78}$

C. $2\overline{)97}$

D. $8\overline{)93}$

E. $7\overline{)94}$

F. $3\overline{)77}$

G. $2\overline{)71}$

H. $5\overline{)76}$

I. $6\overline{)85}$

J. $5\overline{)98}$

K. $4\overline{)90}$

L. $3\overline{)73}$

Unit 6 Test

Division Computation

Read or listen to the question. Use an extra piece of paper to solve the problems. Fill in the circle beside the best answer.

☐ Example:

$4 \times \boxed{} = 24$

$24 \div \boxed{} = 4$

Ⓐ 20   Ⓑ 6
Ⓒ 4   Ⓓ 8

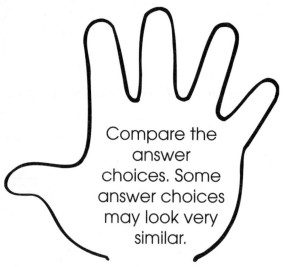

Compare the answer choices. Some answer choices may look very similar.

Answer: B because 4, 6, and 24 make a multiplication and division fact family.

Now try these. You have 20 minutes. Continue until you see ⬡STOP .

---

1. Mark the number sentence that matches the picture.

☆ ☆ ☆ ☆ ☆
☆ ☆ ☆ ☆ ☆
☆ ☆ ☆ ☆ ☆

Ⓐ $5 \div 5$ Ⓑ $15 \div 5$

Ⓒ $5 \div 3$ Ⓓ $10 \div 5$

---

2. Which fact is not part of the same fact family?

| 5×4 | 4×5 | $20 \div 6$ | $20 \div 4$ |
| Ⓐ | Ⓑ | Ⓒ | Ⓓ |

3.

$3\overline{)27}$

| 6 | 7 | 8 | NG |
| Ⓐ | Ⓑ | Ⓒ | Ⓓ |

4.

$9\overline{)81}$

| 7 | 8 | 9 | NG |
| Ⓐ | Ⓑ | Ⓒ | Ⓓ |

GO ON

Unit 6 Test

5. $420 \div 7 =$

6	60	600	NG
Ⓐ	Ⓑ	Ⓒ	Ⓓ

6.

$5\overline{)44}$

8 R4	4 R4	8 R2	9 R1
Ⓐ	Ⓑ	Ⓒ	Ⓓ

7.

$3\overline{)84}$

27 R2	28	28 R1	27 R1
Ⓐ	Ⓑ	Ⓒ	Ⓓ

8.

$4\overline{)97}$

22	23 R3	24 R1	23 R5
Ⓐ	Ⓑ	Ⓒ	Ⓓ

9. The circled number is called the _____.

$14 \div 7 = \text{②}$

Ⓐ quotient   Ⓑ divisor

Ⓒ dividend   Ⓓ factor

10. What is the missing divisor?

○ ○ ○ ○ ○ ○
○ ○ ○ ○ ○ ○
○ ○ ○ ○ ○ ○

Ⓐ 6   Ⓑ 4

Ⓒ 5   Ⓓ NG

$18 \div \square = 6$

GO ON

11. Mark the fact family that does not match the picture.

(A) $12 \div 3 = 4$ (B) $12 \div 4 = 3$

(C) $3 \times 4 = 12$ (D) $4 \times 2 = 8$

12. $36 \div 6 =$

6	4	9	7
(A)	(B)	(C)	(D)

13. $72 \div 8 =$

7	9	8	6
(A)	(B)	(C)	(D)

14.

$6\overline{)300}$

50	80	20	NG
(A)	(B)	(C)	(D)

15.

$7\overline{)37}$

4 R6	6 R3	5 R2	4 R9
(A)	(B)	(C)	(D)

16.

$2\overline{)91}$

43	43 R1	44	45 R1
(A)	(B)	(C)	(D)

17.

$6\overline{)86}$

12	12 R4	14	NG
(A)	(B)	(C)	(D)

GO ON

Teach & Test Math: Grade 3

18. $16 \div 4 =$

   3   4   5   6
   Ⓐ   Ⓑ   Ⓒ   Ⓓ

19.

  $5\overline{)60}$ 12   11 R5   11   10 R5
             Ⓐ   Ⓑ   Ⓒ   Ⓓ

20. What missing number would solve the multiplication and division problems?

  $6 \times \boxed{} = 54$

                 6   7   8   9

  $54 \div \boxed{} = 6$ Ⓐ   Ⓑ   Ⓒ   Ⓓ

Write a 2-digit division problem. Solve the problem.

STOP

Comparing fractions

Unit 7

Fractions are a way to describe equal parts of a whole. They look like this:

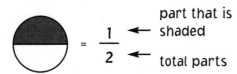

$$\frac{1}{2} \leftarrow \text{part that is shaded}$$
$$\leftarrow \text{total parts}$$

$$\frac{6}{12} \leftarrow \text{parts that are shaded}$$
$$\leftarrow \text{total parts}$$

The interesting part of fractions is that larger numbers do not always mean larger fractions. We can compare fractions using <, >, and =.

$$\frac{1}{3} \, > \, \frac{1}{6}$$

Write a fraction for each picture. Then compare the two fractions using **<**, **>**, or **=**.

$$\frac{1}{3} \, < \, \frac{2}{3}$$

A.

B.

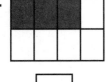 

C.

D.

E.

Name

Adding and subtracting fractions   Unit 7

We have learned that the top and bottom
numbers in a fraction have different
meanings. They also have different names:

$\dfrac{3}{4}$ ← numerator
← denominator

To add or subtract fractions, the denominators must be the same! The denominator in the
answer will also be the same! Add or subtract only the numerators. Here's why:

$\dfrac{1}{3}$ + $\dfrac{1}{3}$ = $\dfrac{2}{3}$ ← added numerators, 1 + 1
← denominator stays the same

Find the sum or difference.

$\dfrac{2}{4} + \dfrac{1}{4} = \dfrac{3}{4}$

A. $\dfrac{6}{8} - \dfrac{4}{8} = \dfrac{\square}{\square}$

B. $\dfrac{1}{5} + \dfrac{3}{5} = \dfrac{\square}{\square}$

C. $\dfrac{4}{10} + \dfrac{5}{10} = \dfrac{\square}{\square}$

D. $\dfrac{7}{8} - \dfrac{5}{8} = \dfrac{\square}{\square}$

E. $\dfrac{9}{10} - \dfrac{3}{10} = \dfrac{\square}{\square}$

F. $\dfrac{6}{9} + \dfrac{2}{9} = \dfrac{\square}{\square}$

G. $\dfrac{10}{12} - \dfrac{6}{12} = \dfrac{\square}{\square}$

H. $\dfrac{68}{100} + \dfrac{12}{100} = \dfrac{\square}{\square}$

I. $\dfrac{42}{100} + \dfrac{36}{100} = \dfrac{\square}{\square}$

                                                            Teach & Test Math: Grade 3

Name

Reducing fractions Unit 7

Some fractions can be renamed, or reduced. Follow these steps to reduce $\frac{9}{12}$:

1. What is the largest number that can be divided into both numbers?

$\frac{9}{12}$

3

2. Divide the numerator and denominator by 3. $\frac{9}{12}\ \begin{matrix}\div 3\\ \div 3\end{matrix} = \frac{3}{4}$ $\frac{9}{12} = \frac{3}{4}$

The amount has not changed, but the fraction has been renamed.

Use what you know about division to reduce these fractions.

$\frac{6}{12}\ \begin{matrix}\div 6\\ \div 6\end{matrix} = \dfrac{\boxed{1}}{\boxed{2}}$

A.

$\frac{4}{10}\ \begin{matrix}\div\\ \div\end{matrix} = \dfrac{\boxed{}}{\boxed{}}$

B.

$\frac{10}{15}\ \begin{matrix}\div\\ \div\end{matrix} = \dfrac{\boxed{}}{\boxed{}}$

C.

$\frac{3}{9}\ \begin{matrix}\div\\ \div\end{matrix} = \dfrac{\boxed{}}{\boxed{}}$

D.

$\frac{8}{12}\ \begin{matrix}\div\\ \div\end{matrix} = \dfrac{\boxed{}}{\boxed{}}$

E.

$\frac{14}{18}\ \begin{matrix}\div\\ \div\end{matrix} = \dfrac{\boxed{}}{\boxed{}}$

F.

$\frac{2}{6}\ \begin{matrix}\div\\ \div\end{matrix} = \dfrac{\boxed{}}{\boxed{}}$

G.

$\frac{2}{4}\ \begin{matrix}\div\\ \div\end{matrix} = \dfrac{\boxed{}}{\boxed{}}$

H.

$\frac{6}{9}\ \begin{matrix}\div\\ \div\end{matrix} = \dfrac{\boxed{}}{\boxed{}}$

I.

$\frac{3}{12}\ \begin{matrix}\div\\ \div\end{matrix} = \dfrac{\boxed{}}{\boxed{}}$

Name

Using fractions as part of a set   Unit 7

Fractions can be used to describe parts of a matching set:

Find $\dfrac{1}{3}$ ● ○ ○   Find $\dfrac{1}{3}$ ● ○ ○
                                              ● ○ ○
                                              ● ○ ○

Sometimes the sets are too
large to draw pictures, so
we can use division again. $\longrightarrow$ 28 ÷ 4 = 7 $\longrightarrow$ $\dfrac{1}{4}$ of 28 = 7

Find $\dfrac{1}{4}$ of 28 means:

Divide 28 into 4 equal groups.

Use division to find the answers.

$\dfrac{1}{3}$ of 21 = $\boxed{7}$

A. $\dfrac{1}{8}$ of 24 = $\boxed{}$

B. $\dfrac{1}{6}$ of 36 = $\boxed{}$

C. $\dfrac{1}{2}$ of 18 = $\boxed{}$

D. $\dfrac{1}{3}$ of 15 = $\boxed{}$

E. $\dfrac{1}{5}$ of 25 = $\boxed{}$

F. $\dfrac{1}{4}$ of 16 = $\boxed{}$

G. $\dfrac{1}{3}$ of 9 = $\boxed{}$

H. $\dfrac{1}{7}$ of 49 = $\boxed{}$

I. $\dfrac{1}{9}$ of 27 = $\boxed{}$

J. $\dfrac{1}{6}$ of 42 = $\boxed{}$

K. $\dfrac{1}{5}$ of 45 = $\boxed{}$

Name

Using decimals

Fractions that are tenths ($\frac{1}{10}$) or hundredths ($\frac{1}{100}$) can be written as a decimal.

Hint: When there are no whole numbers, put a 0 in the ones place.

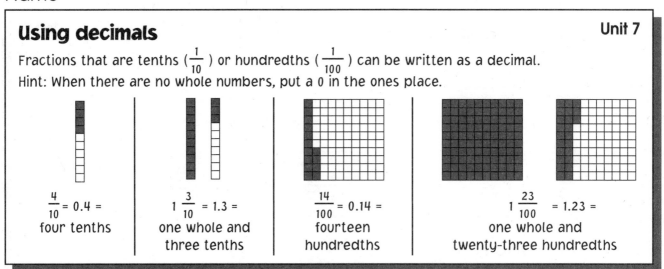

$\frac{4}{10} = 0.4 =$
four tenths

$1\frac{3}{10} = 1.3 =$
one whole and
three tenths

$\frac{14}{100} = 0.14 =$
fourteen
hundredths

$1\frac{23}{100} = 1.23 =$
one whole and
twenty-three hundredths

Write each fraction problem as a decimal number. Color the balloons with tenths blue and the balloons with hundredths green.

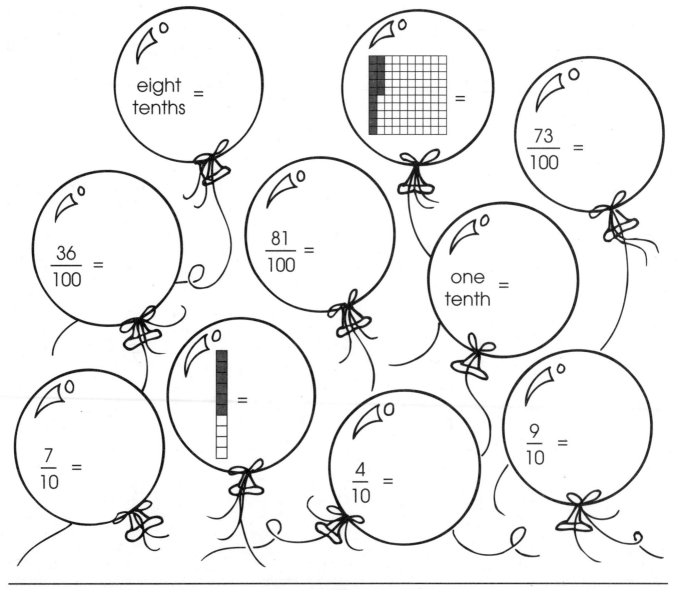

Adding and subtracting decimals

Unit 7

To add and subtract decimals, follow these steps:

1. Line up the decimal points.
2. Add or subtract beginning with the hundredths column, if there are any. Regroup if needed.
3. Add or subtract the tenths column. Regroup if needed.
4. Add or subtract the ones.

Find the sum or difference.

```
    2.4          A.   6.7       B.   3.52
  + 1.8             - 2.9          + 0.78
  ─────             ─────          ──────
    4.2
```

```
C.   2.6        D.   3.66      E.   9.59
   + 5.6           - 0.48         + 0.18
   ─────           ──────         ──────
```

```
F.   8.09    G.   7.3     H.   6.3     I.   1.8     J.   7.34
   + 1.36       - 0.9        - 4.8        + 5.9        - 2.16
   ──────       ─────        ─────        ─────        ──────
```

```
K.   6.03    L.   2.38    M.   4.99    N.   9.4     O.   3.7
   + 1.81       - 0.16       - 2.83       - 0.7        + 3.9
   ──────       ──────       ──────       ─────        ─────
```

Name

Sequencing decimals Unit 7

To sequence decimals with whole numbers like 1, 2, and 3, treat the numbers as decimals. They would be written as 1.0, 2.0, and 3.0. Then we can compare the numbers as usual:

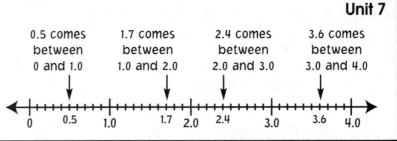

Write the missing numbers.

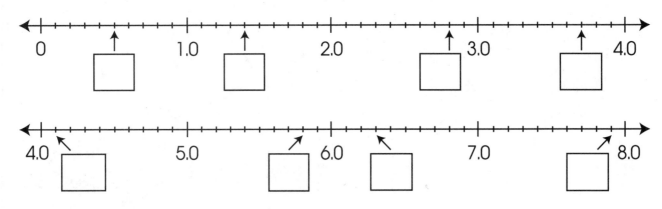

Write the numbers in order from least to greatest. Imagine a number line to help you.

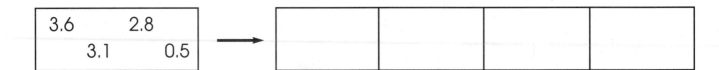

| 0.1 | 1.6 |
| 0.7 | 1.3 |

→

0.1	0.7	1.3	1.6

| 2.4 | 1.9 |
| 0.8 | 0.3 |

→

| 3.6 | 2.8 |
| 3.1 | 0.5 |

→

| 2.6 | 2.1 | 2.8 |
| 1.4 | 0.9 | |

→

Comparing linear measurements

What would you use to measure the distance around your house? What would you use to find the distance to a nearby city? You would probably not use the same unit of measurement for both of these jobs. Listed below are several choices and their comparisons with other units.

Unit	To estimate use:	Comparison
centimeter (cm)	width of your finger	
meter (m)	width of a doorway	equals 1000 cm
kilometer (km)	distance you walk in 15 minutes	equals 1000 m
inch (in.)	width of 2 fingers	
foot (ft.)	height of this paper	equals 12 in.
yard (yd.)	length of a baseball bat	equals 3 ft. or 36 in.
mile	distance you walk in 25 minutes	equals 1,760 yd.

Use the table to find the missing equivalents.

A. 1000 m = _____ km   B. 2 ft. = _____ in.   C. 48 in. = _____ ft.

D. 1 ft. = _____ in.   E. 3 ft. = _____ yd.   F. 2 yd. = _____ ft.

G. 1 yd. = _____ in.   H. 24 in. = _____ ft.   I. 2000 m = _____ km

J. 2 m = _____ cm   K. 4 km = _____ m   L. 36 in. = _____ ft.

Compare using > , < or =.

M. 1 ft. ( ) 1 yd.   N. 1 ft. ( ) 1 in.

O. 4 yd. ( ) 1 mile   P. 1 yd. ( ) 2 ft.

Q. 4 in. ( ) 4 cm   R. 24 in. ( ) 2 ft.

S. 1 ft. ( ) 12 in.   T. 1 mile ( ) 1 km

Name

Reading increments and measuring weight   Unit 7

Have you ever noticed all of the small marks along the top of a scale? They divide the scale into equal increments, or parts. Sometimes the measurement you want is between two numbers which are marked with a smaller line. You must find the increment pattern:

Count by 1s. Shows 44.   Count by 2s. Shows 36.   Count by 5s. Shows 45.

Read each scale. Then circle the best unit of measurement using the weight chart.

Weight Chart

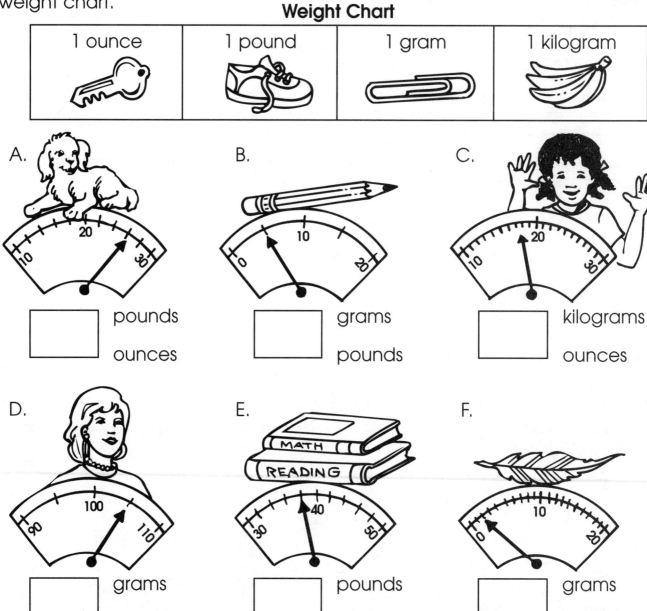

| 1 ounce | 1 pound | 1 gram | 1 kilogram |

A.

☐ pounds
  ounces

B.

☐ grams
  pounds

C.

☐ kilograms
  ounces

D.

☐ grams
  pounds

E.

☐ pounds
  ounces

F.

☐ grams
  pounds

Teach & Test Math: Grade 3

Name

Using measurements of capacity and temperature

Capacity is the amount a container can hold. Standard capacity can be measured in:

1 cup (c.)

1 pint (pt.)
2 cups

1 quart (qt.)
2 pt.
4 c.

1 gallon (gal.)
4 qt.
8 pt.
16 c.

Compare using **<**, **>**, or **=**.

A. 2 c. ◯ 2 gal.   B. 2 pt. ◯ 1 qt.   C. 5 c. ◯ 1 qt.

D. 3 pt. ◯ 2 qt.   E. 3 qt. ◯ 1 gal.   F. 1 gal. ◯ 17 c.

G. 1 gal. ◯ 4 qt.   H. 3 c. ◯ 1 pt.   I. 2 qt. ◯ 4 pt.

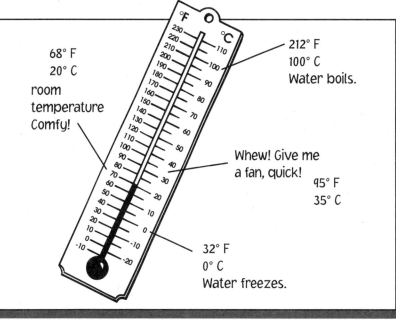

Temperatures can be measured using either side of a thermometer. One side uses Fahrenheit (°F), which is the standard unit of measure. The other side uses Celsius (°C), which is the metric unit of measure.

If you drop below zero, you need to show the temperature using a minus sign.

Example: -23°F

68° F
20° C
room temperature
Comfy!

212° F
100° C
Water boils.

Whew! Give me a fan, quick!
95° F
35° C

32° F
0° C
Water freezes.

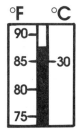
Write the approximate temperature in °F and °C for each thermometer. Then list two articles of clothing you would wear on that day.

_____°F _____°C

I would wear

_____

_____

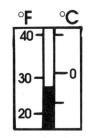

_____°F _____°C

I would wear

_____

_____

Read or listen to the question. Use an extra piece of paper to solve the problems.
Fill in the circle beside the best answer.

Use your time wisely. If something seems difficult, skip it and come back to it later.

❏ Example:

Which of these fractions is the greatest?

Ⓐ $\frac{1}{2}$ Ⓑ $\frac{1}{8}$

Ⓒ $\frac{1}{4}$ Ⓓ $\frac{1}{10}$

Answer: A, because dividing an object into 2 equal parts leaves larger pieces.

Now try these. You have 20 minutes. Continue until you see ⬡STOP.

---

1. The figures below show that:

Ⓐ $\frac{3}{4} > \frac{1}{2}$ Ⓑ $\frac{1}{3} > \frac{1}{2}$

Ⓒ $\frac{3}{4} < \frac{1}{2}$ Ⓓ $\frac{1}{2} < \frac{1}{2}$

---

2. $\frac{4}{10} + \frac{5}{10} = \boxed{}$

$\frac{9}{20}$ $\frac{9}{100}$ $\frac{9}{10}$ NG

Ⓐ   Ⓑ   Ⓒ   Ⓓ

---

3. What fraction of the figure is shaded?

$\frac{1}{6}$ $\frac{1}{2}$ $\frac{1}{3}$ $\frac{1}{4}$

Ⓐ   Ⓑ   Ⓒ   Ⓓ

---

4. $\frac{1}{6}$ of 42 = $\boxed{}$

36   12   24   7

Ⓐ   Ⓑ   Ⓒ   Ⓓ

GO ON ▷

5. $0.25 = \boxed{}$

$\dfrac{25}{10}$ $\dfrac{2}{5}$ $\dfrac{25}{100}$ $\dfrac{250}{100}$

(A)   (B)   (C)   (D)

6.
$$\begin{array}{r} 7.6 \\ +\ 1.4 \\ \hline \end{array}$$

8.0   8.2   9.0   NG

(A)   (B)   (C)   (D)

7. Which decimal on the number line is not correct?

(A)   (B)   (C)   (D)

0   1.7   1.0   1.4   2.0   2.6   3.0   3.5

8. Which statement is not true?

(A) 12 inches = 1 foot   (B) 2 yards = 1 meter

(C) 36 inches = 1 yard   (D) 1 yard = 3 feet

9. What is the closest measurement for the weight of the caterpillar?

(A) 3 grams

(B) 6 pounds

(C) 8 kilograms

(D) 7 grams

10. Which thermometer shows the temperature where Bebe lives?

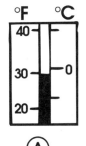 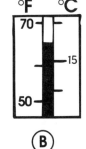 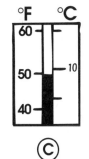 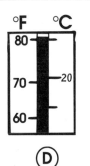

(A)   (B)   (C)   (D)

GO ON

Name

11. Which number sentence is true?

$\frac{1}{2} < \frac{1}{4}$ (A) $\frac{3}{8} < \frac{1}{2}$ (B) $\frac{3}{4} < \frac{1}{2}$ (C) $\frac{1}{3} > \frac{1}{2}$ (D)

12. $\frac{6}{9} + \frac{2}{9} = \boxed{}$

$\frac{8}{18}$ (A) $\frac{8}{9}$ (B) $\frac{9}{18}$ (C) $\frac{9}{8}$ (D)

13. $\frac{8}{24} = \boxed{}$

$\frac{1}{3}$ (A) $\frac{3}{8}$ (B) $\frac{2}{3}$ (C) $\frac{1}{16}$ (D)

14. $\frac{1}{5}$ of $40 = \boxed{}$

8 (A)   2 (B)   16 (C)   NG (D)

15. Which means the same as $1\frac{3}{10}$?

1.03 (A)   3.1 (B)   1.3 (C)   10.3 (D)

16. $\begin{array}{r} 8.63 \\ -\ 2.94 \\ \hline \end{array}$

6.31 (A)   6.79 (B)   5.39 (C)   NG (D)

17. Which point on the number line is 8.3?

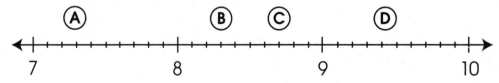

GO ON

18. Which distance is a good estimate for 1 kilometer?

Ⓐ the distance from your classroom to the library

Ⓑ the distance you could walk in 15 minutes

Ⓒ the distance from your garage to the street

Ⓓ the distance you could walk in 60 minutes

19. Mrs. Fritz ordered four steaks from the butcher. What unit of measurement did the butcher probably use to figure out the price for the total weight of the steaks?

grams	cups	liters	pounds
Ⓐ	Ⓑ	Ⓒ	Ⓓ

20. How many quarts equals one gallon?

2	4	6	8
Ⓐ	Ⓑ	Ⓒ	Ⓓ

If chocolate cake is your favorite dessert and your mom offered you a tenth or a hundredth of the cake, which would you choose? Why?

STOP

103

Counting coins

Unit 8

Here are five commonly used coins in the U.S.

    coins

50¢   25¢   10¢   5¢   1¢

The amount coins are worth is called their value. You can find the total value of coins by adding one amount to another amount, which is called counting on.

50¢   75¢   85¢   90¢   95¢   96¢   97¢

Count on to find the total value.

A.
 = [   ] ¢

B.
   = [   ] ¢

C.
 = [   ] ¢

D.
 = [   ] ¢

E.
  = [   ] ¢

F.
     = [   ] ¢

G.
   = [   ] ¢

H.
   = [   ] ¢

Finding values with dollars

Think of a dollar as 100 cents, which means that each dollar is actually 100 equal parts.
That means:

1 penny = $\frac{1}{100}$ = $0.01   1 dime = $\frac{10}{100}$ = $0.10   1 dollar = 1 whole = $1.00

Write each total value using a decimal point and dollar sign.

A.
_____

B.
_____

C.
_____

D.
_____

E.
_____

F.
_____

G.
_____

H.
_____

I.
_____

J.
_____

Name

Comparing values of coins

Unit 8

Have you noticed that values of money can be made using different combinations of coins?
For instance:

 = 25¢    = 25¢    = 25¢

Use the value of coins to complete
the equations.

5 nickels = _____1_____ quarter

A. 50 pennies = _____ dimes

B. 1 dollar = _____ quarters

C. 4 half dollars = _____ dollars

D. 10 dimes = _____ nickels

E. 2 quarters = _____ nickels

F. 50 pennies = _____ nickels

G. 3 dollars = _____ quarters

H. 6 quarters = _____ dimes

I. 2 dimes = _____ pennies

✶ Tell two ways to make each total value.

$2.50 = __2 dollars, 2 quarters__ or ____10 quarters____

J. $1.00 = _____ or _____

K. $0.75 = _____ or _____

L. $1.25 = _____ or _____

Name

Calculating change   Unit 8

Have you ever paid for something and been given change back?
The cashier figures your change using these steps:

       4 9 10

      $5.0.0

1. Begin with the amount you paid the cashier.

    −   0.75

2. Subtract the amount you owe from the amount you paid.

    $4.25

3. The difference is your change.

Find the amount of change that is owed to the customer.

Paid $6.00 Owe − 2.10 $3.90	**A.** Paid $20.00 Owe − 16.20
B. Paid $8.00 Owe − 3.95	**C.** Paid $10.00 Owe − 4.60
D. Paid $9.00 Owe − 8.50	**E.** Paid $5.00 Owe − 0.95
F. Paid $16.00 Owe − 15.15	**G.** Paid $25.00 Owe − 5.00
H. Paid $2.00 Owe − 1.19	**I.** Paid $4.00 Owe − 3.95
J. Paid $10.00 Owe − 7.49	**K.** Paid $12.00 Owe − 11.23

Name

Problem solving using addition and subtraction   Unit 8

The problems you see on this page tell a story. Your job is to use information from the story to make a math problem and solve the problem. This is called **problem solving**. Read each story carefully and ask yourself if it makes sense to add or subtract.

Smokey Joe's Barbecue

MAIN DISHES	SIDE DISHES	BEVERAGES
Eye-Watering Ham ..$3.50	Flame Fries $1.10	Cola $0.75
Burning Hot Ribs........$3.75	Sizzlin' Salad.............$1.05	Lemonade $0.85
Rockin' Roast Beef ..$4.25	Tasty Tater Tots........$0.95	Milk..............................$0.95

A. Ariel ordered ribs and lemonade. How much will her lunch cost?

B. Michael ordered roast beef. He paid with a five dollar bill. How much change will he get?

C. Jonah has $4.08. He buys ham as a main dish. How much does Jonah have left?

D. Terone wonders, "How much does an order of ribs, fries, and a cola cost?"

E. How much more is roast beef than milk?

F. Tracy buys lemonade for herself and three friends. How much does she spend?

G. Ryan spent $5.55 for lunch. He got $0.45 back as change. How much did Ryan start out with?

H. Kelsey orders the least expensive item from each section of the menu. How much does she spend?

Name

Problem solving using multiplication

Some story problems can be answered using multiplication. They ask you to find a total number, similar to addition. The difference is that these stories involve equal sets. For example:

Matthew orders
3 ice cream cones.
Each cone has 2 scoops.
How many scoops of ice cream
did Matthew order?

3	x	2	=	6
number of sets		number in each set		total 6 scoops

Read each story. Would it make sense to add, subtract, or multiply? Find the answers.

A. Bev's 3 guinea pigs ate 24 seeds each. How many seeds did the guinea pigs eat?

B. We found 6 spider webs. Each web had trapped 17 bugs. How many bugs were trapped?

C. A ticket to the game costs $26.00. Amy has $18.00. How much more does Amy need to buy a ticket?

ROW 5
SEAT 18

D. Our class ate 9 pizzas. Each pizza had 12 slices. How many pieces of pizza did our class eat?

E. We passed 8 trucks on the highway. Each truck honked 4 times. How many honks did the trucks make in all?

F. Haley has 52 dimes in her bank. She has 39 nickels. How many coins does she have?

G. Jon is making lemonade for 16 people. Each glass needs 3 spoons of mix. How many spoons of lemonade mix will Jon use?

H. Alonzo has 6 rolls of pennies. Each roll holds 50 pennies. How many pennies does Alonzo have?

109

Name

Problem solving using division | Unit 8

Other story problems can be answered using division. They ask you to find missing parts or make smaller groups. They also involve making equal sets, like these:

Yasmine started with 9 hair ribbons. She split them evenly between 3 girls. How many ribbons did each girl get?

$$9 \div 3 = 3$$
total number ribbons
of groups

Read each story. Would it make sense to add, subtract, multiply, or divide? Find the answers.

A. The Millers have 6 children. When they come to the pool, they bring 36 toys which are equally shared. How many toys does each child get?

B. We found 11 flowers. Each one had 8 petals. How many petals does that make?

C. If a car travels 40 miles per hour, how far can it travel in 3 hours?

D. Mrs. Weitz passes out 24 papers equally to 8 students. How many papers does each child get?

E. Tara and Sira share 12 cookies evenly. How many cookies does each girl get?

F. Luke is coloring eggs. Each container holds 12 eggs. Luke colors 4 containers. How many eggs does Luke color?

G. There are 88 horse legs in the pasture. How many horses are there?

H. We looked under 5 rocks. Each rock had 3 snails underneath. How many snails did we see?

Name

Problem solving with charts

Sometimes a story problem can be answered by creating a chart. For example:

At the end of one week, the grass in Mr. Johnson's yard grew to 3 inches. After two weeks, the grass was 6 inches high. If the pattern continues, how tall will Mr. Johnson's grass be after six weeks?

Week #	1	2	3	4	5	6
Inches Grown	3	6	9	12	15	18

1. Fill in the information from the story.
2. Figure out the pattern
3. Complete the chart using the pattern.

Complete the charts to find the solutions to the problems.

A. Sparky likes to run around Nita's house. It takes him 4 minutes to make it around 2 times. How long will it take Sparky to run around 10 times?

# of circles										
# of minutes										

B. Patsy spends 3 hours every two days practicing her flute. After four days she has spent 6 hours practicing. How many hours will she practice in 12 days?

# of days								
# of hours								

Name _____

Interpreting graphs   Unit 8

Graphs can be used to observe and compare information. The bar graph below shows
the outcome of a science experiment to find the best plant food. The picture graph, also
called a pictograph, shows the number of flowers planted by four classes.

Use the information from the graphs to answer each question.

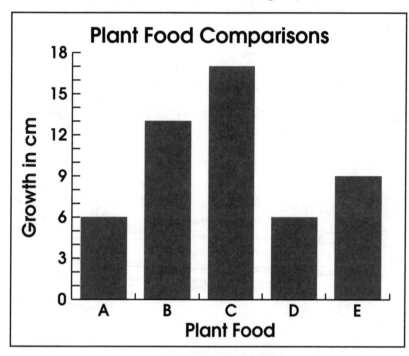

A. How much did Food B's plant grow? _____

B. How much more did Food C's plant grow than Food A's? _____

C. Which two plants show the same growth?
_____ and _____

Flowers We Planted

Rm 102	✿ ✿ ✿ ● ● ●
Rm 103	✿ ✿ ● ● ●
Rm 104	✿ ● ● ● ● ●
Rm 105	✿ ✿ ● ● ● ●

✿ = sun-loving flowers   ● = shade-loving flowers

D. Which two rooms planted the same number of shade-loving flowers?
_____ and _____

E. How many sun-loving flowers were planted? _____

F. Which room planted the same number of each flower? _____

Name

Interpreting a line graph and coordinate grid

Unit 8

The **line graph** below shows points of information. Lines are then drawn between the points to make an easy comparison. This line graph shows the temperature change throughout the week.

Use the points on the graph to find the answers.

High Temperature (°F)

70°
65°
60°
55°
50°

Mon. Tues. Wed. Thurs. Fri.

A. What was the difference in temperature from Wednesday to Friday? _____

B. The temperature rose the most between which two days? _____ and _____

C. What was the lowest temperature reading? _____°F

D. What was the difference in temperature from Monday to Thursday? _____

This is a **coordinate grid**. It is used to show the location of something. The numbers along the bottom and side describe the location using an ordered pair. The first number is from the bottom of the grid, and the second number is from the side of the grid. For example, the raindrop is found at (6, 3). Can you find it?

Draw the symbols found at:

(2, 3) _____

(4, 1) _____

(3, 5) _____

Write the ordered pair:

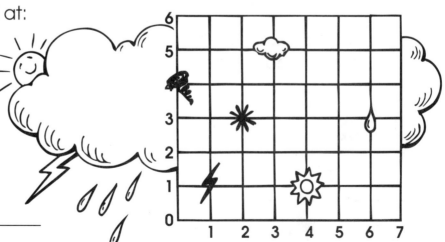

Name

Read or listen to the question. Use an extra piece of paper to solve the problems. Fill in the circle beside the best answer.

❏ **Example:**

What is the value of 1 half dollar, 4 quarters, 2 nickels, and a penny?

$1.26 $2.01 $1.61 $1.86
Ⓐ   Ⓑ   Ⓒ   Ⓓ

Always read the question twice. Does your answer make sense?

Answer: C, because .50 + 1.00 + .10 + .01 = $1.61

Now try these. You have 20 minutes. Continue until you see ⬡STOP⬡.

---

1. Which of these choices would total $3.45?

Ⓐ three dollar bills, four dimes, one nickel

Ⓑ three dollar bills, four nickels, five pennies

Ⓒ two dollar bills, six quarters

Ⓓ two dollar bills, four quarters, five pennies

---

2. What is the total value?

Ⓐ 80¢   Ⓑ 85¢

Ⓒ 90¢   Ⓓ 95¢

---

3. Which set of coins does not total 75¢?

Ⓐ

Ⓑ

Ⓒ

Ⓓ

GO ON ➡

Unit 8 Test

4. How much change is due to the customer?

Paid $10.00
Owe   −   4.40

Ⓐ $6.45   Ⓑ $6.55

Ⓒ $5.45   Ⓓ $5.60

---

5. On Earth Day, the citizens of Greenville planted 326 maple and 269 oak trees. What is the total number of trees that were planted?

157 trees   595 trees   585 trees   57 trees
   Ⓐ   **Ⓑ**   Ⓒ   Ⓓ

---

6. Richard and Nick were playing a video game. Richard won with a score of 92 points. What else do you need to know to figure out Nick's score?

Ⓐ the total amount of time they played

Ⓑ the total of both scores

Ⓒ Nick's bonus points

Ⓓ the name of the video game

---

7. You have 63¢ and gum costs 9¢ per pack. What other information can you figure out using the facts from the story problem?

Ⓐ the type of gum you will buy

Ⓑ the number of friends you can share with

Ⓒ the number of pieces of gum in each pack

Ⓓ the number of packs you can buy

---

8. From this chart you know:

Ⓐ Jacob read 16 books in 4 days.

Ⓑ Jacob read 2 books each day.

Ⓒ Jacob will read 22 books in 5 days.

Ⓓ Jacob will read 25 books.

Day	1	2	3	4
Books	4	8	12	16

GO ON

9. What is the total value of the coins and bills?

(A) $2.25   (B) $2.76

(C) $2.80   (D) $2.85

Use this graph to answer questions 10 and 11.

Book Reports

Carly	🗋 🗋 📕 📕 📕
Lindsay	📕 🗋 🗋 📕 📕 🗋 🗋 🗋 🗋 🗋
Ben	📕 📕 📕 🗋 🗋 📕 📕
Greg	🗋 🗋 📕 📕 🗋 🗋 🗋 📕 🗋

🗋 = fiction

📕 = nonfiction

10. Which student read the same number of each type of book?

Carly (A)   Lindsay (B)   Ben (C)   Greg (D)

11. To find the total number of nonfiction books that were read, you would do which of the following?

(A) Count Carly's and Ben's shaded books.

(B) Count all of the shaded books.

(C) Count all of the non-shaded books.

(D) Count the total number of books.

12. Which amount does not total a dollar?

(A) 1 half dollar, 1 quarter, 1 nickel   (B) 4 quarters

(C) 1 half dollar, 2 quarters   (D) 2 half dollars

GO ON

13. Which group of coins has the greatest value?

Ⓐ   Ⓑ   Ⓒ   Ⓓ

14. Parker spent $8.07 at the school store. What information do you need to know to figure out Parker's change?

Ⓐ the items that Parker bought

Ⓑ the amount of money Parker paid

Ⓒ the price of lunch

Ⓓ the number of sale items that are included

15. Grandma made nine pies for the fair. She used six apples per pie. How many apples did Grandma use?

| 54 apples | 48 apples | 56 apples | 45 apples |
| Ⓐ | Ⓑ | Ⓒ | Ⓓ |

16. The ballet class learned three dances for their recital. Each dance had fifty-three steps. How many steps did the class learn?

| 59 steps | 63 steps | 56 steps | 159 steps |
| Ⓐ | Ⓑ | Ⓒ | Ⓓ |

17. Lilly jumped over a rope 48 times in 4 minutes. How many jumps did she make each minute?

| 14 jumps | 24 jumps | 12 jumps | 16 jumps |
| Ⓐ | Ⓑ | Ⓒ | Ⓓ |

GO ON ⟩

18. Farmer Gray's chicken eggs are hatching! On the first day, 4 eggs hatched. On the next day, 8 eggs had hatched. If the pattern continues, how many eggs will be hatched by the fifth day?

16 eggs	20 eggs	22 eggs	24 eggs
Ⓐ	Ⓑ	Ⓒ	Ⓓ

19. What figure is found at (2, 4)?

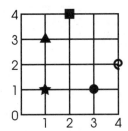

★ Ⓐ   ℮ Ⓑ   ▲ Ⓒ   ■ Ⓓ

20. What is the ordered pair for the ● ?

(1, 4)	(3, 1)	(4, 1)	(1, 3)
Ⓐ	Ⓑ	Ⓒ	Ⓓ

As a science project, Stephen fed three types of food to his guinea pig, Fuzzy. Stephen found that Fuzzy ate 10 sesame seeds, 7 corn kernels, and 8 pellets. Create a bar graph to show Stephen's results.

STOP

Final Review Test Name Grid

Write your name in pencil in the boxes along the top. Begin with your last name. Fill in as many letters as will fit. Then follow the columns straight down and bubble in the letters that correspond with the letters in your name. Complete the rest of the information the same way. You may use a piece of scrap paper to help you keep your place.

STUDENT'S NAME		SCHOOL

LAST — FIRST — MI

TEACHER

FEMALE ○   MALE ○

DATE OF BIRTH

MONTH	DAY	YEAR

Bubble grid letters A–Z in name columns.

Date of Birth bubbles:
JAN ○, FEB ○, MAR ○, APR ○, MAY ○, JUN ○, JUL ○, AUG ○, SEP ○, OCT ○, NOV ○, DEC ○

DAY: 0 0, 1 1, 2 2, 3 3, 4, 5, 6, 7, 8, 9

YEAR: 0 0, 1 1, 2 2, 3 3, 4 4, 5 5, 6 6, 7 7, 8 8, 9 9

GRADE ③ ④ ⑤

Final Review Test Answer Sheet

Pay close attention when transferring your answers. Fill in the bubbles neatly and completely. You may use a piece of scrap paper to help you keep your place.

SAMPLES
A ⒶⒷ**Ⓒ**Ⓓ
B Ⓕ**Ⓖ**ⒽⒿ

1 ⒶⒷⒸⒹ	7 ⒶⒷⒸⒹ	13 ⒶⒷⒸⒹ	19 ⒶⒷⒸⒹ	25 ⒶⒷⒸⒹ
2 ⒻⒼⒽⒿ	8 ⒻⒼⒽⒿ	14 ⒻⒼⒽⒿ	20 ⒻⒼⒽⒿ	26 ⒻⒼⒽⒿ
3 ⒶⒷⒸⒹ	9 ⒶⒷⒸⒹ	15 ⒶⒷⒸⒹ	21 ⒶⒷⒸⒹ	27 ⒶⒷⒸⒹ
4 ⒻⒼⒽⒿ	10 ⒻⒼⒽⒿ	16 ⒻⒼⒽⒿ	22 ⒻⒼⒽⒿ	28 ⒻⒼⒽⒿ
5 ⒶⒷⒸⒹ	11 ⒶⒷⒸⒹ	17 ⒶⒷⒸⒹ	23 ⒶⒷⒸⒹ	29 ⒶⒷⒸⒹ
6 ⒻⒼⒽⒿ	12 ⒻⒼⒽⒿ	18 ⒻⒼⒽⒿ	24 ⒻⒼⒽⒿ	30 ⒻⒼⒽⒿ

Name

Final Review Test

Read or listen to the question. Use an extra piece of paper to solve the problems and to keep your place on the score sheet. Fill in the circle beside the best answer completely and neatly.

❑ Example:

Find the product.

$$\begin{array}{r} 5 \\ \times\ 6 \\ \hline \end{array}$$

Ⓐ 31

Ⓑ 25

Ⓒ 36

Ⓓ NG

Answer: D because the answer 30 is not given.

Now try these. You have 30 minutes.

Continue until you see ⬡STOP .

Remember your Helping Hand Strategies:

 1. When using scratch paper, copy carefully.

 2. Compare the answer choices. Some answer choices may look very similar.

 3. Use your time wisely. If something seems difficult, skip it and come back to it later.

 4. Always read the question twice. Does your answer make sense?

---

1. Which of these numbers shows a nine in the ones place and a four in the hundreds place?

459	954	495	945
Ⓐ	Ⓑ	Ⓒ	Ⓓ

---

2. Mark the number sentence that does not mean the same as 5 x 3.

Ⓕ 3 + 3 + 3 + 3 + 3   Ⓖ 3 x 5

Ⓗ 3 + 5   Ⓙ 5 + 5 + 5

3.

$160 \div 4 = \boxed{}$

4	6	40	60
Ⓐ	Ⓑ	Ⓒ	Ⓓ

GO ON ➤

4.

$\frac{1}{4}$ of 20 = ☐

15
(F)

5
(G)

24
(H)

NG
(J)

5. Sam is learning to build towers of blocks. He will stack 6 blocks on each tower. He has 54 blocks. How many towers can Sam build?

6 towers
(A)

7 towers
(B)

8 towers
(C)

9 towers
(D)

6. Round the numbers in the box to the nearest ten. How many of them equal 740?

| 735 | 749 | 725 | 728 | 741 |

(F) 2   (G) 3

(H) 4   (J) 5

7.

7 x 8 = ☐

48
(A)

49
(B)

54
(C)

56
(D)

8.

5 ⟌ 27

5 R4
(F)

5 R2
(G)

4 R2
(H)

4 R1
(J)

9. Which figure shows more than 1/2 shaded?

(A)

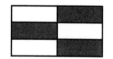

(B)

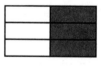

(C)

(D)

10. Which group of money is worth a different amount than all of the others?

(F) 1 dollar, 3 dimes, 5 pennies

(G) 5 quarters, 2 dimes, 1 nickel

(H) 5 quarters, 10 pennies

(J) 4 quarters, 3 dimes, 5 pennies

GO ON ▷

Final Review Test

11. If the perimeter of the figure equals 1 yard, how long is the missing side?

☐ in.

8 in.　　　8 in.

5 in.

(A) 12 in.

(B) 15 in.

(C) 18 in.

(D) NG

12.

$$\begin{array}{r} 56 \\ \times\ \ 3 \\ \hline \end{array}$$

152　　158　　164　　NG
(F)　　(G)　　(H)　　(J)

13. Which problem does not equal four?

28 ÷ 7　　　32 ÷ 8　　　27 ÷ 9　　　24 ÷ 6
(A)　　　　　(B)　　　　　(C)　　　　　(D)

14.

$$\begin{array}{r} \$3.09 \\ 2.45 \\ +\ \ 0.72 \\ \hline \end{array}$$

$5.26　　$6.16　　$6.26　　NG
(F)　　　(G)　　　(H)　　　(J)

15.

$\dfrac{45}{100} + \dfrac{17}{100} = $ ☐

0.62　　0.28　　0.47　　NG
(A)　　(B)　　(C)　　(D)

16. How much more money is in the first purse than in the third purse?

(F) $0.39

(G) $0.49

(H) $0.41

(J) $0.28

GO ON

Final Review Test

17. What number is missing in the sequence below?

38, 42, ☐ , 50

43   44   45   NG
Ⓐ   Ⓑ   Ⓒ   Ⓓ

18.
$$167 \times 5$$

535   835   805   NG
Ⓕ   Ⓖ   Ⓗ   Ⓙ

19. The clock shows the time it is now. Isabelle's piano lesson starts in 20 minutes. What time is her lesson?

Ⓐ 10:00   Ⓑ 11:15

Ⓒ 6:15   Ⓓ 6:00

20. The circled number is called the _____.

$18 \div 2 = ⑨$

Ⓕ dividend   Ⓖ factor

Ⓗ product   Ⓙ quotient

21. Which sentence is not true of these figures?

Ⓐ They both have a line of symmetry.

Ⓑ They are the same size.

Ⓒ They have been rotated.

Ⓓ They are congruent.

22.
$$647 - 128$$

609   519   529   621
Ⓕ   Ⓖ   Ⓗ   Ⓙ

GO ON

23. Kayla is filling party bags. She will put seven pieces of candy in each bag. What other information will help Kayla decide how much candy she needs?

(A) the sale price of the candy

(B) the date of the party

(C) the number of bags to fill

(D) the theme of the party

24.

$$
\begin{array}{r}
5,462 \\
+ \ 1,539 \\
\end{array}
$$

6,991   6,981   7,021   7,001

(F)   (G)   (H)   (J)

This line graph shows the number of visitors to the zoo during certain times of the day. Use it to answer question 25.

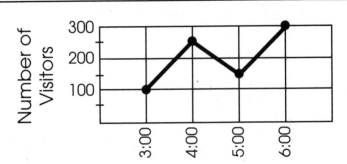

25. What was the difference in the number of visitors between 3:00 and 6:00?

200   150   100   50

(A)   (B)   (C)   (D)

26.

$6\overline{)89}$ 15   14 R5   13 R11   NG

              (F)   (G)   (H)   (J)

GO ON

Final Review Test

27.

$$5000 + 300 + 60 + 9 = \boxed{}$$

Ⓐ 5,639   Ⓑ 9,635

Ⓒ 5,069   Ⓓ 5,369

28. Find the area of the figure.

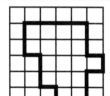

Ⓕ 20 sq. units   Ⓖ 17 sq. units

Ⓗ 18 sq. units   Ⓙ 19 sq. units

29. Which figure has two sets of parallel line segments?

Ⓐ   Ⓑ   Ⓒ   Ⓓ

30. What unit of measurement would you use to measure the weight of a bug?

pound   gram   centimeter   pint
Ⓕ   Ⓖ   Ⓗ   Ⓙ

hamburger..........$4.50   French fries..........$1.25   lemonade $0.75
hot dog...............$2.25   cookie ....$0.50   shake $1.00

Choose three items from the menu. What is the total amount? What bills and coins could you use to pay?

⬡ STOP

Answer Key

Page 5

A. 5th, 6th, 7th, 8th, 9th, 10th, 11th; B. 21st, 22nd, 23rd, 24th, 26th, 27th, 28th; C. 80th, 81st, 82nd, 84th, 85th, 86th, 87th, 89th; D. 7; E. 5; F. 12th

Page 6

Classroom: Students should draw 6 pencils, 3 books, 4 balls, and 5 apples.; Beach: Students should draw 8 fish, 2 starfish, 3 shovels, and 4 shells.

Page 7

A. 63; B. 78; C. 51; D. 2; 5. 90; E. 19; F. 86

Page 8

A. 403; B. 510; C. 154; D. 237; E. 309; F. 600; G. 170

Page 9

A. 1,253; B. 2,075; C. 2,000; D. 2,300; E. 1,009

Page 10

A. 2,000 + 300 + 50 + 8; B. 1,000 + 400 + 0 + 7; C. 900 + 20 + 1; D. 7,000 + 800 + 0 + 0; E. 3,000 + 200 + 60 + 4; F. 5,000 + 100 + 80 + 2; G. 600 + 10 + 4; H. 4,000 + 0 + 70 + 3; I. 9,000 + 500 + 30 + 0

Page 11

ON HIS FEET!

Page 12

74, 75, 76, 77, 78, 79, 80, 81, 82, 83, 84, 86, 87, 89, 90, 91, 93, 94, 95, 97, 98, 99; 323, 324, 325, 327, 328, 329, 331, 332, 334, 335, 336, 338, 339, 340, 342, 343, 344, 346, 347, 348, 349, 350; 672, 673, 674, 675, 677, 678, 679, 681, 682, 684, 685, 686, 687, 688, 689, 690, 692, 693, 694, 696, 697, 698, 699, 881, 883, 884, 886, 887, 888, 890, 891, 892, 893, 895, 896, 897, 898, 900, 903, 904, 905, 907, 908, 909, 910

Page 13

A. 0, 4, 8, 12; B. 0, 6, 12; C. 33, 36, 39, 42, 45; D. 62, 64, 66, 68, 70, 72, 74; E. 84, 88, 92, 96

Page 14

A. 3, 6, 9, 12, 15; B. 6, 12, 18; C. 2, 4, 6, 8, 10, 12, 14, 16; D. 7, 14, 21; E. 9, 18, 27; F. 5, 10, 15, 20

Unit 1 Test

1. C; 2. B; 3. C; 4. B; 5. D; 6. B; 7. A; 8. C; 9. A; 10. A; 11. D; 12. D; 13. B; 14. C; 15. C; 16. D; 17. B; 18. D; 19. A; 20. B; Constructed-response answers will vary.

Page 19

A. 6,911; B. 4,073; C. 9,207; D. 839; E. 9,601; F. 8,390; G. 417; H. 5,082; I. 470; J. 3,512; K. 6,914

Page 20

Number orders may vary.

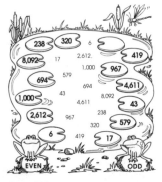

Page 21

440; 720; 1,950; 260; 3470; 990; 2,920; 810; 420; 600; 50

Page 22

700; 100; 600; 300; 700; 900; 700; 500; 900

Page 23

A. <, >, <, >, <, <; B. <, >, >, <, >, <

Page 24

A. 905, 730, 340, 172; B. 2,314, 1,170, 800, 512; C. 6,000, 4,000, 982, 960; D. 490, 472, 436, 401; E. 17, 71, 87, 107; F. 19, 96, 600, 906; G. 1,900, 2,700, 4,350, 7,000; H. 200, 620, 2,600, 6,200

Page 25

A. 35, 7:00, 7:35; 10, 8:00, 8:10; 5, 10:00, 10:05; 30, 5:00, 5:30; B. 15, 2:00, 2:15; 55, 9:00, 9:55; 50, 4:00, 4:50; 45, 6:00, 6:45; 5, 12:00, 12:05

Page 26

Phrases may vary. Possible answers include: quarter after 9:00; quarter till 2:00; noon;

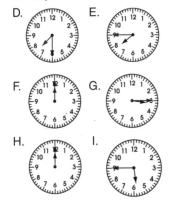

Page 27

Page 28

A. 50 minutes: B. 1 hour 40 minutes; C. 9:20; D. 1 hour 10 minutes; E. 11:15

Unit 2 Test

1. B; 2. C; 3. C; 4. A; 5. B; 6. D; 7. A; 8. D; 9. C; 10. B; 11. A; 12. D; 13. B; 14. C; 15. D; 16. C; 17. A; 18. C; 19. B; 20. C; Constructed-response answers will vary.

Page 33

A. cone, 1; B. cylinder, 2; C. sphere, 0; D. rectangular prism, 6; E. pyramid, 5; F. cube, 6; G. cylinder, 2; H. sphere, 0; I. pyramid, 5; J. cone, 1; K. rectangular prism, 6

Page 34

A. 4, 4, 4, yes, no; B. 3, 3, 3, no, no; C. 4, 4, 4, yes, no; D. 0, 0, 0, no, yes; E. 4, 4, 4, yes, yes; F. 5, 5, 5, no, no; G. 0, 2, 0, no, no

Page 35

A. flip; B. no; C. turn/rotate; D. slide; E. no; F. flip; G. flip; H. turn/rotate; I. no

Page 36

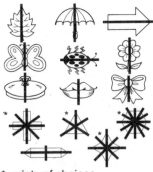

*variety of choices

Page 37

A. 24 units; B. 10 units; C. 24 inches; D. 16 cm; E. 21 miles; F. 32 miles

Page 38

A. 8 sq. cm; B. 10 sq. cm; C. 10 sq. cm; D. 8 sq. cm; E. 16 sq. cm; F. 7 sq. cm; G. 12 sq. cm; H. 11 sq. cm; I. 22 sq. cm

Page 39

A. 7 cubic units; B. 11 cubic units; C. 5 cubic units; D. 6 cubic units; E. 7 cubic units; F. 8 cubic units; G. 10 cubic units; H. 12 cubic units; I. 10 cubic units

Page 40

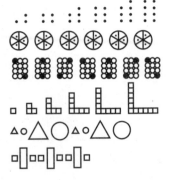

Unit 3 Test

1. A; 2. D; 3. C; 4. D; 5. B;
6. A; 7. D; 8. B; 9. D; 10. B;
11. C; 12. C; 13. A; 14. B;
15. A; 16. B; 17. C; 18. D;
19. A; 20. C; Constructed-
response answers will vary.

Page 46

A. 3,619; B. 5,798; C. 5,986;
D. 7,797; E. 6,995; F. 4,689;
G. 8,948; H. 7,786

Page 47

A. 85; B. 82; C. 90; D. 68;
E. 31; F. 50; G. 635; H. 777;
I. 949; J. 817; K. 368;
L. 5,176; M. 3,216; N. 7,397;
O. 1,777

Page 48

A TAXICAB DRIVER!

Page 49

A. $11.37; B. $12.23;
C. $13.50; D. $16.53; E.
$10.58; F. $13.34; G. $18.08;
H. $19.04; I. $6.63; J. $12.70;

The kingdom with the castle
on the left is most wealthy.

Page 50

A. 1,132; B. 6,241; C. 7,324;
D. 4,153; E. 1,355; F. 5,221;
G. 2,240; H. 4,353

Page 51

A. 5 T, 14 O; B. 7 T, 10 O; C. 0
T, 12 O; D. 3 T, 15 O; E. 6 T,
18 O; F. 8 T, 16 O; G. 2, T; 13
O; H. 0 H, 15 T, 6 O; I. 6 H, 11
T, 3 O; J. 8 H, 17 T, 2 O; K. 4
H, 10 T, 3 O; L. 4 Th, 10 H, 3
T, 7 O; M. 7 Th, 14 H, 5 T, 1
O; N. 8 Th, 11 H, 2 T, 6 O

Page 52

A. 26; B. 66; C. 18; D. 18; E.
56; F. 27; G. 742; H. 332; I.
472; J. 394; K. 331; L. 1,773;
M. 1,780; N. 5,713; O. 5,913

Page 53

A. 3,729; B. 1,589; C. 3,820;
D. 8,858; E. 2,612; F. 8,768;
G. 485; H. 3,805; I. 7,388; J.
5,321; K. 458; L. 774; M.
2,479

Page 54

		7	2	6		
			2	7	8	0
	1	4	2	1		
			6			
		5	1	3		
				5		
		7	0	5	3	
6	0	8				
		4	4	1	6	
					7	
					6	
			1	8	8	
			5			
			4			
			4			

Page 55

A. 310 + 900 = 1,210; B. 360 -
140 = 220; C. 840 + 260 =
1,100; D. 920 - 470 = 450; E.
650 + 210 = 860; F. 500 + 700
= 1,200; G. 400 - 200 = 200;
H. 200 + 800 = 1,000; I. 900 -
300 = 600; J. 800 - 700 = 100

Unit 4 Test

1. B; 2. C; 3. D; 4. A; 5. A; 6. B;
7. B; 8. A; 9. C; 10. D; 11. D;
12. A; 13. B; 14. C; 15. A; 16.
B; 17. D; 18. B; 19. C; 20. A;
Constructed-response
answers will vary.

Midway Review Test

1. B; 2. H; 3. A; 4. H; 5. D; 6. F;
7. A; 8. J; 9. B; 10. J; 11. C;
12. G; 13. D; 14. J; 15. C;
16. G; 17. D; 18. J; 19. B;
20. H; Constructed-response
answers will vary.

Page 66

A. 5 + 5 + 5 = 15, 3 x 5 = 15;
B. 3 + 3 = 6, 2 x 3 = 6; C. 2 +
2 + 2 + 2 = 8, 4 x 2 = 8; D. 4 +
4 = 8, 2 x 4 = 8; E. 3 + 3 + 3 =
9, 3 x 3 = 9; F. 4 + 4 + 4 = 12,
3 x 4 = 12; G. 2 + 2 + 2 = 6, 3
x 2 = 6; H. 5 + 5 = 10, 2 x 5 =
10

Page 67

0, 0, 0, 0; 6, 9, 7, 2; 8, 10, 6,
8; 9, 6, 15, 12; 8, 4, 16, 24; 5,
30, 15, 40; 12, 42, 24, 18; 14,
56, 35, 42; 24, 40, 48, 64; 27,
54, 63, 81

Page 68

A. 24, 6, 24, 64; B. 48, 63, 45,
9; C. 15, 28, 16, 72; D. 36, 21,
25, 12; E. 18, 56, 10, 54; F.
32, 16, 27, 12; G. 49, 81, 14,
20; H. 30, 40, 10, 35; I. 36,
18, 9, 4

Page 69

YOUR RIGHT ELBOW!;
BECAUSE FISH HAVE
THEIR OWN SCALES!

Page 70

A. 189; B. 640; C. 126; D. 549;
E. 144; F. 637; G. 208; H. 219;
I. 360; J. 106; K. 355; L. 368;
M. 189; N. 728; O. 164

Page 71

A. 335; B. 296; C. 406; D. 576;
E. 171; F. 150; G. 496; H. 448;
I. 245; J. 207; K. 498; L. 846;
M. 456; N. 656

Page 72

A. 756; B. 1,062; C. 2,684;
D. 1,500; E. 4,272; F. 878;
G. 1,330; H. 900; I. 8,199;
J. 708; K. 2,223; L. 1,488;
M. 814; N. 1,155; O. 1,740

Page 73

A. $36.50; B. $27.28;
C. $24.72; D. $43.05;
E. $1.36; F. $7.92; G. $21.72;
H. $14.95; I. $9.59; J. $8.19;
K. $24.00; L. $11.07; M.
$.088; N. $11.46; O. $2.96;
P. $47.60

Unit 5 Test

1. C; 2. D; 3. B; 4. C; 5. A;
6. B; 7. D; 8. A; 9. A; 10. D;
11. C; 12. B; 13. C; 14. A;
15. B; 16. D; 17. A; 18. A;
19. D; 20. C; Constructed-
response answers will vary.

Page 78

A. 2; B. 5; C. 2; D. 4; E. 3; F. 3;
G. 2; H. 6; I. 2

Page 79

A. 4; B. 3; C. 4; D. 5; E. 5; F. 3;
G. 3; H. 6; I. 5; J. 9; K. 5; L. 2;
M. 4; N. 2; O. 6

Page 80

A. 6; B. 8; C. 4; D. 3; E. 3; F. 6;
G. 3; H. 5; I. 3; J. 3; K. 5; L. 4;
M. 9; N. 9; O. 7; P. 9; Q. 8; R.
7; S. 8; T. 6

Page 81

A. 1; B. 6; C. 8; D. 6; E. 9; F. 8;
G. 2; H. 4; I. 7; J. 7; K. 6; L. 9;
M. 1; N. 7; O. 6; P. 9; Q. 4; R.
4; S. 9; T. 9; U. 7; V. 9; W. 7;
1819

Page 82

A. 50; B. 90; C. 50; D. 90;
E. 90; F. 30; G. 60; H. 60; I. 60;
J. 60; K. 40; L. 10; M. 40;
N. 90; O. 30; P. 20; Q. 50

Page 83

A. 6 R2; B. 9 R4; C. 5 R2; D. 3
R2; E. 8 R2; F. 7 R5; G. 9 R2;
H. 6 R3; I. 4 R3; J. 4 R4; K. 9
R7; L. 5 R6; M. 3 R5; N. 6 R6;
O. 3 R3

Page 84

A. 49; B. 18; C. 12; D. 15;
E. 29; F. 12; G. 38; H. 14; I. 18;
J. 24; K. 17

Page 85

A. 29 R2; B. 19 R2; C. 48 R1;
D. 11 R5; E. 13 R3; F. 25 R2;
G. 35 R1; H. 15 R1; I. 14 R1;
J. 19 R3; K. 22 R2; L. 24 R1

Unit 6 Test

1. B; 2. C; 3. D; 4. C; 5. B;
6. A; 7. B; 8. C; 9. A; 10. D;
11. D; 12. A; 13. B; 14. A;
15. C; 16. D; 17. D; 18. B;
19. A; 20. D; Constructed-
response answers will vary.

Page 90

A. 2/4 = 4/8; B. 3/8 < 1/2;
C. 1/3 = 2/6; D. 3/4 > 2/4;
E. 1/2 < 3/4

Page 91

A. 2/8; B. 4/5; C. 9/10; D. 2/8;
E. 6/10; F. 8/9; G. 4/12;
H. 80/100; I. 78/100

Answer Key

Page 92
A. 2/5; B. 2/3; C. 1/3; D. 2/3;
E. 7/9; F. 1/3; G. 1/2; H. 2/3;
I. 1/4

Page 93
A. 3; B. 6; C. 9; D. 5; E. 5; F. 4;
G. 3; H. 7; I. 3; J. 7; K. 9

Page 94

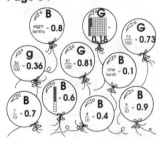

Page 95
A. 3.8; B. 4.30; C. 8.2; D. 3.18;
E. 9.77; F. 9.45; G. 6.4; H. 1.5;
I. 7.7; J. 5.18; K. 7.84; L. 2.22;
M. 2.16; N. 8.7; O. 7.6

Page 96
0.5, 1.4, 2.8, 3.7; 4.1, 5.8,
6.3, 7.9; 0.3, 0.8, 1.9, 2.4;
0.5, 2.8, 3.1, 3.6; 0.9, 1.4,
2.1, 2.6, 2.8

Page 97
A. 1; B. 24; C. 4; D. 12; E. 1;
F. 6; G. 36; H. 2; I. 2; J. 2000;
K. 4000; L. 3; M. <; N. >; O. <;
P. >; Q. >; R. =; S. = T. >

Page 98
A. 26 pounds; B. 5 grams;
C. 18 kilograms; D. 105
pounds; E. 38 ounces; F. 2
grams

Page 99
A. <; B. = ; C. >; D. <; E. <;
F. <; G. =; H. >; I. =; 88°F,
33°C, Possible answers
include: shorts, T-shirts,
sandals; 28°F, -3°C, hat, coat,
gloves

Unit 7 Test
1. A; 2. C; 3. B; 4. D; 5. C;
6. C; 7. A; 8. B; 9. D; 10. A;
11. B; 12. B; 13. A; 14. A;
15. C; 16. D; 17. B; 18. B;
19. D; 20. B; Constructed-
response answers will vary.
Tenth, because that is a
bigger piece.

Page 104
A. 82¢; B. 43¢; C. 95¢; D. 81¢;
E. 85¢; F. 86¢; G. 29¢; H. 45¢

Page 105
A. $1.76; B. $1.03; C. $1.13;
D. $3.55; E. $1.25; F. $2.00;
G. $2.15; H. $2.50; I. $1.50;
J. $3.05

Page 106
A. 5; B. 4; C. 2; D. 20; E. 10;
F. 10; G. 12; H. 15; I. 20;
Answers will vary for J–L.
Possible answers include:
J. 4 quarters, 2 half dollars;
K. 3 quarters, 7 dimes and 1
nickel; L. 5 quarters, 4
quarters and 5 nickels

Page 107
A. $3.80; B. $4.05; C. $5.40;
D. $.50; E. $4.05; F. $.85;
G. $20.00; H. $.81; I. $.05;
J. $2.51; K. $.77

Page 108
A. $4.60; B. $.75; C. $.58;
D. $5.60; E. $3.30; F. $3.40;
G. $6.00; H. $5.20

Page 109
A. 72 seeds; B. 102 bugs;
C. $8.00; D. 108 pieces;
E. 32 honks; F. 91 coins;
G. 48 spoons of mix; H. 300
pennies

Page 110
A. 6 toys; B. 88 petals; C. 120
miles; D. 3 papers; E. 6
cookies; F. 48 eggs; G. 22
horses; H. 15 snails

Page 111
A. 20; B. 18

Page 112
A. 13 cm; B. 11 cm; C. A and
D; D. Rm 102 and Rm 103;
E. 8; F. Rm 102

Page 113
A. 6°; B. Thursday and Friday;
C. 50°; D. 10°; (2, 3) =
snowflake; (4, 1) = sun; (3, 5)
= cloud; (1, 1); (0, 4)

Unit 8 Test
1. A; 2. C; 3. D; 4. D; 5. B;
6. B; 7. D; 8. A; 9. D; 10. B;
11. B; 12. A; 13. D; 14. B;
15. A; 16. D; 17. C; 18. B;
19. D; 20. B; Constructed-
response answers will vary.
Check students' bar graphs.

Final Review Test
1. A; 2. H; 3. C; 4. G; 5. D;
6. F; 7. D; 8. G; 9. A; 10. G;
11. B; 12. J; 13. C; 14. H; 15.
A; 16. F ; 17. D; 18. G; 19. C;
20. J; 21. A; 22. G; 23. C; 24.
J; 25. A; 26. G; 27. D; 28. G;
29. D; 30. G; Constructed-
response answers will vary.